CAMPAIGN 359

STALINGRAD 1942–43 (1)

The German Advance to the Volga

ROBERT FORCZYK

ILLUSTRATED BY STEVE NOON
Series editor Nikolai Bogdanovic

OSPREY PUBLISHING
Bloomsbury Publishing Plc

Kemp House, Chawley Park, Cumnor Hill, Oxford OX2 9PH, UK
29 Earlsfort Terrace, Dublin 2, Ireland
1385 Broadway, 5th Floor, New York, NY 10018, USA
Email: info@ospreypublishing.com
www.ospreypublishing.com

OSPREY is a trademark of Osprey Publishing Ltd

First published in Great Britain in 2021
Transferred to digital print in 2023

A catalogue record for this book is available from the British Library.

Print ISBN: 978 1 4728 4265 7
ePub: 978 1 4728 4266 4
ePDF: 978 1 4728 4263 3
XML: 978 1 4728 4264 0

Maps by www.bounford.com
3D BEVs by Paul Kime
Index by Janet Andrew
Typeset by PDQ Digital Media Solutions, Bungay, UK
Printed and bound in Great Britain by CPI (Group) UK Ltd,
Croydon CR0 4YY

24 25 26 27 28   10 9 8 7 6 5 4

MIX
Paper | Supporting
responsible forestry
FSC® C013604

Addendum

Image acknowledgements showing as (Nik Cornish@www.stavka.org)
on pages 5, 18, 19 (twice), 22, 38, 39, 45, 48, 49, 57, 76, 81, 84, 85, 89,
should read as (Nik Cornish@www.stavka.org.uk).

Artist's note

Readers may care to note that the original paintings from which the
colour plates in this book were prepared are available for private sale.
All reproduction copyright whatsoever is retained by the publishers.
All enquiries should be addressed to the artist, via the following website:

https://www.steve-noon.co.uk

The publishers regret that they can enter into no correspondence upon
this matter.

The Woodland Trust

Osprey Publishing supports the Woodland Trust, the UK's leading
woodland conservation charity.

To find out more about our authors and books visit
www.ospreypublishing.com. Here you will find extracts, author
interviews, details of forthcoming events and the option to sign up for
our newsletter.

Acronyms

ARMIR	Armata Italiana in Russia (Italian Army in Russia)
BAD	Bombardirovochnaya Aviatsionnaya Diviziya (Bomber Aviation Division)
BAP	Bombardirovochnyi Aviatsionnyi Polk (Bomber Aviation Regiment)
CCNN	Camicie Nere (Blackshirts)
GKO	Gosudarstvennyj Komitet Oborony (State Defence Committee)
GRU	Glavnoye Razvedyvatel'noye Upravleniye (the Red Army's military intelligence directorate)
IAD	Isrebitelnyi Aviatsionnyi Division (Fighter Aviation Division)
IAK	Isrebitelnyi Aviatsionnyi Korpus (Fighter Aviation Corps)
IAP	Isrebitelnyi Aviatsionnyi Polk (Fighter Aviation Regiment)
NKVD	Narodnyy Komissariat Vnutrennikh Del (People's Commissariat for Internal Affairs)
OKH	Oberkommando des Heeres (Supreme High Command of the German Army)
ORAP	Otdel'nyy Razvedyvatel'nyy Aviatsionnyy Polk (Independent Reconnaissance Aviation Regiment)
OTB	Otdel'nyy Tankovyy Batal'on (Independent Tank Battalion)
PADA	Principe Amedeo Duca d'Aosta
PVO	Protivovozdushnoy Oborony (Air Defence Command)
RVGK	Rezerv Verkhovnogo Glavnokomandovaniya (STAVKA reserve)
ShAD	Shturmovoy Aviatsionnyi Division (Ground Attack Aviation Division)
ShAP	Shturmovoy Aviatsionnyi Polk (Ground Attack Aviation Regiment)
SPW	Schützenpanzerwagen (armoured infantry vehicle)
STZ	Stalingradski Traktorni Zavod (Stalingrad Tractor Works)
VS	Verbrauchssatz (unit of measure for fuel)
VVS	Voyenno-Vozdushnye Sily (Soviet Air Force)

Key to unit symbols

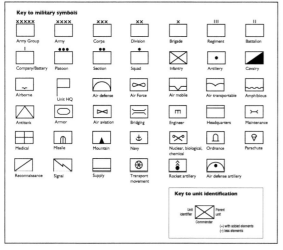

PREVIOUS PAGE
German PzKpfw IV tanks, probably from 16.Panzer-Division, during
the fighting in the great bend of the Don River, mid-August 1942.
(Süddeutsche Zeitung, 00384540)

CONTENTS

ORIGINS OF THE CAMPAIGN

Adolf Hitler had spelled out his intent to crush the Soviet Union and gain *Lebensraum* (living room) for the German people in its conquered territories in his prewar book, *Mein Kampf*. He regarded communism as a mortal threat to his nascent Third Reich, and intended to remove it from the Earth, permanently. However, just prior to the start of World War II, Hitler was forced by economic and strategic circumstances to strike a temporary bargain with his bête noire, Josef Stalin. Through the Molotov–Ribbentrop Pact, the Third Reich and the Soviet Union became temporary accomplices in dividing up spheres of influence in Eastern Europe, as well as establishing a trade relationship to thwart the expected Anglo-French blockade. Hitler then invaded Poland, and Stalin eventually moved in to occupy eastern Poland. Thanks to the Molotov–Ribbentrop Pact, Hitler could afford to turn all his military strength against the West and crush France in a six-week campaign in 1940. Once the French were defeated and the English driven from the Continent, Hitler then turned his eyes towards achieving his paramount goal: the destruction of the Soviet Union. Operation *Barbarossa* was intended to demolish the Soviet Union's military capacity with an all-out campaign. Both Hitler and the Oberkommando des Heeres (OKH) staff who planned *Barbarossa* expected the main objectives to be completed within about three months, although it was assumed that limited mop-up operations would continue for some time afterwards.

Operation *Barbarossa* began on 22 June 1941, with three German army groups crossing the Soviet border. Having refined their air–ground manoeuvre tactics in Poland and the West, the German army groups sliced through the Soviet border defences and advanced rapidly, encircling and smashing unprepared Red Army units along the way. The Red Army put up stout resistance at Smolensk, Kiev and Leningrad, but Soviet losses were enormous. Indeed, the Soviets

had put their strongest forces in the South-Western Front to defend Kiev, but, nevertheless, Heeresgruppe Süd captured Kiev on 19 September and smashed the South-Western Front in the largest double envelopment in military history. Stalin sent Marshal Semyon K. Timoshenko to lead the remnants of the Red Army in the eastern Ukraine, which withdrew towards the Donbass. On 24 October, Heeresgruppe Süd captured Kharkov, and continued to press eastwards. Yet despite achieving unprecedented operational-level victories, the Wehrmacht's logistical situation quickly deteriorated as it advanced further into the Soviet Union and German losses mounted. The onset of the muddy period in Russia also slowed the German advance. In one last desperate lunge, Heeresgruppe Süd managed to capture Rostov on 20 November, but Heeresgruppe Mitte was stopped at the outskirts of Moscow. The culmination of Operation *Barbarossa* left the Wehrmacht overextended and vulnerable.

Hitler and Mussolini visit an Italian unit in the Ukraine, 28 August 1941. Generalfeldmarschall Gerd von Rundstedt, commander of Heeresgruppe Süd at the time, stands on the right. In 1942, Hitler asked Mussolini for more troops for the Eastern Front, but only provided him with the barest outline of *Blau*. German–Italian cooperation on the Eastern Front was extremely poor, particularly logistic support, which did nothing to enhance the combat effectiveness of Italian units. (Nik Cornish@www.stavka.org)

Despite suffering nearly 3 million military casualties since the start of *Barbarossa*, the Red Army was still intact and capable of launching a desperate counter-offensive just as the winter weather immobilized the Germans. The Red Army's winter counter-offensive caught the Germans completely off balance, and forced Heeresgruppe Mitte to pull back from the outskirts of Moscow, while Heeresgruppe Süd was forced to abandon Rostov. German human and material losses in the winter retreats were serious, and by the end of the year, the German forces in Russia had suffered 830,000 casualties (including 209,595 dead or missing) and had lost 3,000 tanks. The German operational centre of gravity – their tanks and air support – had been eroded to the point that they barely figured in the desperate winter battles. Indeed, much of the Luftwaffe was pulled back to Germany to regroup, allowing the Soviet Air Force (Voyenno-Vozdushnye Sily, VVS) to regain local air superiority in a few sectors.

From Stalin's point of view, the invaders appeared to be on the verge of dissolution, as Napoleon's retreating armies had, and he pressed his generals to expand the scope of the winter counter-offensive, attacking on each front with whatever forces were available. Instead of a well-planned, coordinated counter-offensive, the Soviet winter attacks degenerated into a series of pell-mell offensive pulses between January and March 1942, which consumed the limited reserves available. With his forces in retreat, Hitler ordered that his armies stand fast and adopt hedgehog-style defensive tactics, based on key towns and cities. Given that the Red Army had lost most of its tanks and heavy artillery in the first six months of the war, the Soviets were able to encircle some German units, but they could not destroy them. In the south, Timoshenko's South-Western Front threatened to recapture Kharkov,

The massive losses suffered by Timoshenko's disastrous Kharkov offensive in May 1942 set the stage for *Fall Blau* by weakening the Red Army's forces in the eastern Ukraine. In little over a month of fighting, the South-Western Front lost over 300,000 troops, which left Timoshenko's command vulnerable against the resurgent Heeresgruppe Süd. (Author's collection)

but only succeeded in creating a bulge in Heeresgruppe Süd's front known as the Barvenkovo salient. By March 1942, it was clear that the Wehrmacht was beginning to recover its balance and the Soviet counter-offensives had run out of steam.

An unusual lull settled over most of the Eastern Front in April 1942, as both sides planned their next moves to regain the initiative. Both sides chose to mount new offensives in the Kharkov sector. Stalin ordered Timoshenko to attack out of the Barvenkovo salient before the German 6.Armee was ready to start its own offensive. Timoshenko's offensive, begun on 12 May 1942, seriously stressed General Friedrich Paulus' 6.Armee for a week, but failed to retake Kharkov. However, the German counter-offensive that began on 17 May, designated Operation *Fridericus*, proved devastating (see Osprey Campaign No. 254 *Kharkov 1942: The Wehrmacht Strikes Back*). Heeresgruppe Süd managed to encircle and destroy the bulk of the Soviet assault group in a *Kesselschlacht* (cauldron battle), which cost the South-Western Front over 277,000 casualties. Soviet material losses in the failed offensive were serious, including 775 tanks, 1,646 artillery pieces and 542 aircraft. Even worse, Heeresgruppe Süd followed up *Fridericus* with two subsequent local offensives, which further knocked the South-Western Front off balance. Operation *Wilhelm*, conducted between 10 and 15 June, attempted to encircle the Soviet 28th and 38th armies east of Kharkov; although both Soviet armies escaped the trap, 6.Armee mauled them and gained valuable ground. Between 22 and 25 June, Generaloberst Ewald von Kleist's 1.Panzer-Armee conducted Operation *Fridericus II* against the right flank armies of the Southern Front. As a result of both operations, the Germans had captured another 47,000 Soviet troops and gained an excellent jumping-off position along the Oskol River to begin their main summer offensive. Soviet industry was still recovering and could not immediately replace these losses, temporarily leaving Timoshenko's much-depleted South-Western Front in a vulnerable state. The stage was now set for the main German offensive of 1942 – *Fall Blau* (*Case Blue*)– which was intended to demolish the Soviet Union's ability to continue the war.

This is the first volume in a trilogy that will cover the entire Stalingrad campaign from June 1942 until February 1943. Volume 1 covers *Fall Blau* and the German advance to the Volga. Volume 2 will cover the fighting in and around Stalingrad between September and November 1942, while Volume 3 will cover the Soviet counter-offensive, from November 1942 to February 1943. Operations in the Caucasus, already covered in Osprey Campaign No. 281, *The Caucasus 1942–43: Kleist's Race for Oil*, will only be discussed in passing in this trilogy.

CHRONOLOGY

1942

5 April	Führer Directive No. 41 issued, laying out the objectives for the German summer offensive.
29 May	Heeresgruppe Mitte begins planning *Fall Kreml* (*Kremlin*) deception operation.
10–15 June	The 6.Armee conducts Operation *Wilhelm*, which defeats the Soviet 28th Army around Volchansk.
19 June	Through an accident, the Soviets acquire the plans for *Fall Blau* (*Case Blue*), but judge them to be a deception.
22–26 June	The 6.Armee conducts Operation *Fridericus II* against the South-Western Front, resulting in the capture of Kupyansk.
28 June	*Fall Blau* begins with 4.Panzer-Armee attacking the Bryansk Front.
29 June–2 July	4.Panzer-Armee defeats the Bryansk Front's armoured reserves in large-scale tank battles west of Voronezh.
30 June	6.Armee attacks the South-Western Front.
4 July	4.Panzer-Armee captures a bridge over the Don River.
6 July	4.Panzer-Armee captures Voronezh.
	5th Tank Army begins its unsuccessful counter-attack against 4.Panzer-Armee.
	Stavka authorizes Timoshenko's armies to withdraw.
7 July	The Voronezh Front is created.
9 July	The northern wing of Heeresgruppe Süd is redesignated as Heeresgruppe B.
11 July	Führer Directive No. 43 assigns 4.Panzer-Armee to Heeresgruppe A.
12 July	The Stalingrad Front is created.
15 July	Generalfeldmarschall Fedor von Bock is relieved of command of Heeresgruppe Süd.
21 July	Timoshenko is relieved of command of the Stalingrad Front.
22 July	Führer Directive No. 45 is issued, outlining new goals for Operation *Braunschweig*.
24 July	The XIV.Panzer-Korps crushes the right flank of the 62nd Army.
26 July	The Stalingrad Front launches a counter-offensive with the 1st and 4th Tank armies against 6.Armee in the Don Bend.

28 July	Stavka Order No. 227 issued: *Ni Shagu Nazad*! (Not a step back!)
4 August	Stavka creates a new South-Eastern Front under General-polkovnik Andrei I. Eremenko.
7 August	The Germans encircle the 62nd Army and part of the 1st Tank Army in the Don Bend.
13 August	General-leytenant Vasily N. Gordov is relieved of command of the Stalingrad Front, Eremenko takes over.
17 August	The 6.Armee crosses the Don at Vertyachii.
18 August	The Soviet 1st Guards Army establishes a bridgehead across the Don at Kremenskaya.
23 August	The XIV.Panzer-Korps crosses the Don at Vertyachii, and its 16.Panzer-Division reaches the Volga River north of Stalingrad.
23–24 August	Massive Luftwaffe bombing raids on Stalingrad.
25 August	The 6.Armee captures Kalach.
29 August	The Soviet 64th Army is defeated, opening the south-west approaches to Stalingrad.

OPPOSING COMMANDERS

GERMAN

Hitler's sacking of Generalfeldmarschall Walther von Brauchitsch, commander-in-chief of the Heer (army), in December 1941 removed the last buffer between the Führer's mercurial style of decision making and the army's field commanders. Thereafter, Hitler arrogated the role of army commander-in-chief unto himself, although he still left the actual staff work to the OKH staff, led by Generaloberst Franz Halder. Unlike during *Barbarossa*, Hitler now felt empowered to give orders directly to army-level commands (and below), when the spirit moved him. In addition to Hitler's increased meddling in field operations, the Ostheer (German Army in the East) was afflicted by a sudden shortage of

competent operational-level leaders. Hitler had relieved a number of senior commanders, such as Fedor von Bock, Heinz Guderian and Gerd von Rundstedt, after the failure of *Barbarossa*, and he had a tendency to replace them with officers who were obsequious, rather than aggressive. The sudden death of Generalfeldmarschall Walther von Reichenau in January 1942 created a serious gap in German operational-level leadership in the southern theatre of Russia. Von Reichenau, who was one of the few really aggressive senior German commanders in the East, had turned over 6.Armee to Paulus in December 1941, and moved up to take command of Heeresgruppe Süd. After von Reichenau's death, Hitler needed a competent, experienced field commander to lead *Blau*, and he had few options. He chose to reinstate von Bock.

Generalfeldmarschall Fedor von Bock (1880–1945) took command of Heeresgruppe Süd on 20 January 1942. Von Bock was a professional infantry officer and the most experienced operational-level commander in the Wehrmacht in early 1942, having successfully led an army group in Poland in 1939, in the Western campaign of 1940 and Heeresgruppe Mitte during *Barbarossa*. Von

General der Panzertruppe Friedrich Paulus, commander of 6.Armee, was tasked with the capture of Stalingrad. Paulus had limited field command experience and proved himself a mediocre commander during the prior Kharkov campaign in May. His selection for command of the drive on Stalingrad was a serious mistake by Hitler. (Süddeutsche Zeitung, 00006368)

Bock was not a charismatic commander, but he was methodical and was comfortable in directing large formations. Taking command of the overextended Heeresgruppe Süd during the middle of the enemy's winter counter-offensive, von Bock was able to stabilize the front and achieve a decisive victory in the Battle of Kharkov in May 1942. Although von Bock was loyal to Hitler, he was not subservient, and tended to argue with him about priorities and objectives – matters that Hitler felt he alone should decide. Consequently, Hitler's relationship with von Bock deteriorated during the early stages of *Blau*, even though the operation was progressing well. Eventually, Hitler found sufficient reason to relieve von Bock of command on 13 July 1942; von Bock never received another command during the war.

Generaloberst Maximilian von Weichs (1881–1954) was made commander of 2.Armee in October 1939. Von Weichs had commanded 2.Armee during the French and Yugoslav campaigns, as well as the initial phase of Operation *Barbarossa* in 1941. He was a Bavarian cavalryman by training, and was given command of 1.Panzer-Division when it formed in 1935, which helped advance his career. By 1942, von Weichs was a very experienced army-level commander, but he had primarily served in supporting roles and had not gained much first-hand experience of mechanized warfare. Nor was von Weichs noted as a particularly aggressive commander; he lacked the offensive zeal of someone like von Reichenau. After von Bock was sacked, Hitler gave von Weichs command of the northern part of Heeresgruppe Süd, which had been redesignated as Heeresgruppe B. As army group commander, von Weichs had difficulty controlling his dispersed forces, and did not show any flair for manoeuvre warfare.

General der Panzertruppe Friedrich Paulus (1890–1957) was made commander of 6.Armee in January 1942. Paulus had made his reputation in the Heer as a diligent, hard-working staff officer, not as a field commander. Indeed, Paulus' prior command experience was negligible – he had never commanded a division or corps. Although Paulus was involved in the planning of *Barbarossa*, he did not participate in the operation, and lacked direct experience of fighting the Red Army. During the Battle of Kharkov in May 1942, Paulus turned in a mediocre command performance, and von Bock judged him to be indecisive in moments of crisis. Given the Wehrmacht's reputation for competent battlefield leadership, it is indicative of the Ostheer's dire shortage of command cadre that Paulus was not relieved prior to *Blau*. One explanation is that Hitler had grown tired of aggressive but argumentative field commanders, such as Guderian, and was satisfied with army commanders who could simply obey his orders from the Wolfsschanze (Wolf's Lair); Paulus excelled in that regard.

Generaloberst Hermann Hoth (1885–1971) took command of 4.Panzer-Armee on 15 May 1942. Hoth was a Prussian infantryman and General Staff-trained officer who rose steadily through the ranks of the Wehrmacht in the 1930s. He ably led the XV.Armee-Korps (mot.) during the Polish and French campaigns, then Panzergruppe 3 during *Barbarossa* in 1941. Hoth managed to avoid being sacked by Hitler during the winter battles and was given command of 17.Armee, helping to stabilize the southern front after the loss of Rostov. By 1942, Hoth was one of the most experienced and aggressive German operational-level manoeuvre commanders, and he knew how to get the best out of his *Panzer-Divisionen*. Indeed, Hoth demonstrated great operational command skill during the opening weeks of *Blau*, marking him as one of the best German manoeuvre commanders of World War II. He also knew how to work well with other commanders and to avoid trying to debate directives from Hitler. However, Hoth was frustrated by chronic logistical problems during the campaign.

Generaloberst Hermann Hoth, commander of 4.Panzer-Armee. Hoth achieved a major tactical victory at Voronezh, but afterwards, Hitler failed to recognize what had been achieved and proceeded to micromanage and fragment Hoth's command. (Süddeutsche Zeitung, 00013260)

The Luftwaffe's contribution to *Blau*, Luftflotte 4, was initially commanded by Generaloberst Alexander Löhr, but he turned the formation over to **Generaloberst Wolfram Freiherr von Richthofen (1895–1945)** on 4 July 1942. Von Richthofen, a Prussian aristocrat, was a World War I ace and cousin of the famous 'Red Baron', Manfred von Richthofen. Hermann Göring brought von Richthofen into the Luftwaffe in 1933 and he served with Legion Condor in Spain in 1937, where he began to experiment with close air support tactics. During the Polish campaign, von Richthofen developed a reputation for 'terror bombing', first directing his Ju 87 Stukas to bomb the defenceless town of Wieluń and later Warsaw, which resulted in heavy civilian loss of life. Afterwards, his command was redesignated as VIII.Fliegerkorps, which he led in the Western campaign and *Barbarossa*. Von Richthofen developed his command into the premier close air support force in the Luftwaffe, and was consistently used to reinforce the main effort in every German offensive. Von Richthofen was an aggressive commander, who was not shy in inserting himself into decisions on ground battles, as well. Hitler admired von Richthofen's ruthless attitude towards war, and respected his competence in aviation operations. However, von Richthofen's frequent criticism of army operations led to friction with ground commanders, particularly Hoth.

Marshal Semyon K. Timoshenko, commander of the South-Western Front in June 1942. Despite a strong prewar reputation and good political ties with Stalin, Timoshenko proved a mediocre front-level commander and was repeatedly defeated in 1941 and 1942. By July 1942, Stalin lost patience with Timoshenko's incompetence and relieved him of command, although he was kicked upstairs into high-level desk jobs for the rest of the war. (Author's collection)

General-leytenant Vasily N. Gordov, commander of the Stalingrad Front for three weeks in July and August 1942. He was given the near-impossible task of stopping 6.Armee's advance, and when he failed, he was summarily relieved of command. (Author's collection)

SOVIET

In the Red Army, operational-level decision-making authority resided in front- and army-level military councils, with political commissars holding veto power over military commanders. **Nikita S. Khrushchev (1894–1971)** was the senior commissar in the South-Western Front, then the Stalingrad Front, during *Blau*. **Alexey S. Chuyanov (1905–77)**, head of the Communist Party organization in Stalingrad, also played a significant role in front-level decision making. At the strategic level, Soviet dictator Josef Stalin and his Stavka headquarters staff set out the objectives for all major military operations and directed subordinate fronts to plan the actual details. Stalin's purges of 1937–41 had left deep scars in the senior Red Army command cadre, which in 1941 and 1942 meant that inexperienced officers were often thrust into high-level command slots. Consequently, Stavka sent senior staff officers, such as General Georgy Zhukov and General-polkovnik Aleksandr Vasilevsky, to help fronts coordinate critical operations.

Marshal Semyon K. Timoshenko (1895–1970) took command of the South-Western Front after the disastrous defeat at Kiev in September 1941. Timoshenko was a career cavalryman with strong personal ties to Stalin, which enabled him to survive the purges in the 1930s and to rise to the position of People's Commissar of Defence in 1940. However, Timoshenko had almost no formal military training, and did not understand modern military technology or mechanized warfare, which made him rather timid as a front-level commander. On the defence, Timoshenko demonstrated at Smolensk in 1941 that he could make a stand against the Wehrmacht's best effort, but his one offensive operation, the attack on Kharkov in May 1942, was a complete fiasco. By the time that *Blau* began, Stalin had lost confidence in Timoshenko, and relieved him of command on 21 July 1942. Timoshenko was replaced by **General-leytenant Vasily N. Gordov (1896–1950)**, who briefly commanded the Stalingrad Front, before he was relieved of command on 12 August 1942 for failure to stop the German advance. Stalin was famous for nursing grudges against individuals who offended him, and after the war, Stalin had Gordov executed, ostensibly for making critical remarks about the dictator. Stalin sent **General-polkovnik Andrei I. Eremenko (1892–1970)**, another of his favoured cavalry officers, to take command of the Stalingrad Front. Eremenko had been wounded twice during the 1941 campaign, and was still recovering when recalled to the front. Nevertheless, Eremenko put in a solid performance during the Battle of Stalingrad.

General-leytenant Filipp I. Golikov was commander of the Bryansk Front at the beginning of *Blau*, before he briefly took over the newly formed Voronezh Front. Golikov had been in charge of the GRU, the Red Army's military intelligence directorate, at the start of the war. After the German invasion began, he was sent as head of the Red Army's military delegation to London in July 1941. Although Golikov fumbled the initial response to *Blau*, he was politically adept and survived, eventually rising to Marshal of the Soviet Union by 1961. (Author's collection)

General-leytenant Filipp I. Golikov (1900–80) was commander of the Bryansk Front, which suffered much of the initial shock of *Blau*. On 12 July, Golikov took command of the newly formed Voronezh Front, but **General-polkovnik Aleksandr Vasilevsky (1895–1977)** – chief of Stavka's General Staff – arrived soon thereafter and assumed effective command over the front until October. Nevertheless, Golikov played a major role in both the Stalingrad and Voronezh fronts for the duration of the campaign. Golikov had been the head of the GRU (the Red Army's military intelligence directorate) at the start of *Barbarossa* and had relatively limited command experience, but he was an astute political soldier.

The Bryansk Front was supported by the 2nd Air Army, led by **General-major Stepan Krasovskiy (1897–1983)**, while the South-Western/Stalingrad Front was supported by the 8th Air Army, led by **General-major Timofei T. Khriukhin (1910–53)**. Khriukhin was a prototypical 'new Soviet man', who had risen from being a labourer to a party member, then a bomber pilot. He gained combat experience in Spain and China during the late 1930s. By the age of 32, Khriukhin was in command of one of the first air armies in the VVS, and he supported the adoption of new tactics to improve the tactical efficiency of his squadrons.

OPPOSING FORCES

GERMAN

The German formations from Heeresgruppe Süd (soon to be redesignated as Heeresgruppe B) that would advance towards Voronezh and Stalingrad – 2.Armee, 6.Armee and 4.Panzer-Armee – initially numbered over 600,000 personnel and comprised some of the most combat-effective troops in the Ostheer in mid-1942. A total of 34 German divisions were committed in the initial phase of *Blau*, equipped with about 30,000 motor vehicles and 80,000 horses. Yet it is highly significant that neither the Ostheer nor the OKH had any significant operational reserves to provide Heeresgruppe Süd. Furthermore, both air and ground units committed to *Blau* were tired after months of continuous combat, and did not have a significant period to rest or refit prior to the beginning of the new offensive. Nevertheless, overall German front-line morale was excellent after the recent victory at Kharkov, and the troops believed that the campaign would decide the war in Russia.

Infantry
Heeresgruppe B would require a great deal of infantry to seize its objectives and then hold the new front along the Don and Volga. By mid-1942, the

German infantry advance eastwards, July 1942. The Wehrmacht still had a significant amount of high-quality, veteran infantry to support another major offensive, but the Ostheer was no longer able to replace heavy losses in a timely manner. Most German troops in mid-1942 were confident of victory in the campaign, and willing to make the sacrifices required for final victory. A few weeks in Stalingrad put paid to that initial optimism. (Bundesarchiv, Bild 101I-217-0465-32A, Foto: Klintzsch)

OKH's inability to fully replace personnel losses led to most of the infantry divisions in the Ostheer being reduced to three regiments of two battalions, yielding a total of just six infantry battalions per division. However, the infantry divisions in Heeresgruppe B were the exception, and most still retained the three battalion per regiment structure. Nevertheless, von Bock's infantry divisions started *Blau* at an average of about 75 per cent authorized strength. In LV.Armee-Korps, 45.Infanterie-Division started the campaign with 70 per cent of its infantry, 95.Infanterie Division with 93 per cent of its infantry and 299.Infanterie-Division with 83 per cent. Amazingly, once the campaign began, Heeresgruppe B had the lowest priority for personnel replacements, behind even Heeresgruppe Nord. During July and August 1942, Heeresgruppe B received only one replacement for every 2.8 losses. In order to make up some of the personnel shortfall, German units were already resorting to using Soviet prisoners as auxiliary volunteers (*Hilfswilliger*, or Hiwis) in their support units; 299.Infanterie-Division listed 1,122 Hiwis in its ranks at the start of *Blau*. It is also noteworthy that Heeresgruppe B possessed only a single Waffen-SS unit, the 1.SS-Infanterie-Brigade (mot.); this reinforced brigade had 4,853 troops, but was not fully motorized and its artillery was horse-drawn.

In terms of equipment, the German infantry was just beginning to receive the excellent MG 42 machine gun, although most units were equipped with the MG 34 or older machine guns for the duration of *Blau*. German infantry divisions had begun to receive a mix of improved anti-tank weapons, such as the 7.5cm Pak 97/38 or 7.5cm Pak 40, but still relied heavily upon the older 3.7cm and 5cm Pak guns. The real firepower of the infantry divisions resided in their artillery regiments, which were supposed to have 36 10.5cm guns and 12 15cm howitzers. In some units, captured Soviet anti-tank guns and artillery pieces were incorporated to make up shortfalls. In terms of mobility, the German infantry divisions suffered from insufficient motor transport and were too dependent upon horses to move their artillery and supplies. Heeresgruppe B had a total of about 252 German infantry battalions. Of these, just three were *Gepanzert* (armoured) battalions, provided with SPW half-tracks (in the 3., 9. and 23.Panzer divisions). Another 24 battalions were motorized, in the four motorized infantry divisions. However, the remaining 89 per cent of the infantry walked, which meant they could not keep up with the *Panzer-Divisionen*. In a pursuit operation, such as the early days of *Blau*, the German infantry could march 30–40km per day across open steppe, but this left the troops increasingly exhausted by the time they reached their objectives.

Armour

Blau was based upon the Ostheer's ability to conduct mechanized warfare in conjunction with close air support. The Panzer and motorized infantry divisions in Heeresgruppe B were the cutting edge, intended to slice through the Soviet front lines as they had in 1941 and then encircle and annihilate the entrapped foes in *Kesselschlacht* (cauldron battles). Three of the five *Panzer-Divisionen* in Heeresgruppe B were veteran formations, but the 23. and 24.Panzer divisions were new units, which had only recently arrived on the Eastern Front. By mid-1942, the Ostheer knew that it had a winning operational formula, which was revalidated at Kharkov in May. Yet, in technical terms, the Germans had been chagrined during *Barbarossa* to

An armoured (*Gepanzert*) *Panzergrenadier-Kompanie* mounted in SPW half-tracks advances across the steppe. Those *Panzer-Divisionen* chosen for *Blau* were given a battalion of armoured infantry, which substantially increased the combat power of vanguard units. The Germans also used the SdKfz 251 half-track to carry 8cm mortars and other infantry support weapons, as well. (Bundesarchiv, Bild 101I-218-0511-22, Foto: Thiede)

discover that the Red Army had two tanks – the T-34 and KV-1 – which were clearly superior to the existing German PzKpfw III and IV medium tanks. Consequently, the OKH had been obliged to push through a crash programme during the winter of 1941/42 to upgrade its tanks and anti-tank (Panzerjäger) units. By June 1942, this programme was just beginning to bear results, but shortfalls in German armaments production meant that only small amounts of improved weapons would reach the front in time for *Blau*. In the *Panzer-Divisionen*, the PzKpfw IV Ausf. G was introduced in April 1942 with the long-barrelled 7.5cm KwK 40 L/43 gun, while the PzKpfw III Ausf. J and Ausf. L models were equipped with the 5cm KwK 39 L/60 gun.[1] Both upgraded tanks offered much-improved lethality against the T-34, with better range and penetration than the previous models. However, at the start of *Blau*, there were only 546 improved PzKpfw III and 133 PzKpfw IV tanks on the Eastern Front, virtually all of which were in von Bock's Heeresgruppe Süd. Hitler was gambling that fewer than 700 upgraded tanks and German tactical-level proficiency would be sufficient to propel the Third Reich to decisive victory against the Red Army, which by this point had over 4,000 T-34s and KV-1s.

In order to deal with the enemy's overall 4:1 superiority in armour, the OKH also sought to increase the anti-tank capabilities of its assault-gun units (which had been intended for infantry support) and to create specialist self-propelled tank destroyer units. The reliable Sturmgeschütz (Stug) III assault gun was upgraded with a long 75mm gun, and a variant known as the Sturmhaubitze (StuH) 42 was armed with a 10.5cm howitzer.

---

1   The upgraded PzKpfw IV was initially known as the 'Ausf. F2' model, but was redesignated as the Ausf. G model on 1 July 1942.

Heeresgruppe Süd was also provided with three battalions of the new self-propelled tank destroyers, known as the Marder II and Marder III, equipped with the ex-Soviet 76.2mm gun. While these weapons increased Heeresgruppe B's anti-tank capabilities, these weapons were primarily suited to defensive operations, and *Blau* was intended to be a campaign of manoeuvre. Altogether, the OKH deliberately massed its best armoured forces in Heeresgruppe Süd, providing von Bock with 70 per cent of the total German tanks and assault guns on the Eastern Front (32 of 46 *Panzer-Abteilungen* and 13 of 21 *Sturmgeschütz-Abteilungen*).

Luftwaffe

At the start of *Blau*, Luftflotte 4 had over 1,100 operational aircraft, with virtually all of its bombers in IV.Fliegerkorps, while VIII.Fliegerkorps was a combined-arms force. Despite heavy losses of equipment and manpower in the previous 12 months of the Russian campaign, the Luftwaffe units on the Eastern Front started *Blau* at the apex of their tactical and operational capabilities. In particular, the veteran *Jagdflieger* (fighter pilots) in the eight *Jagdgruppen* (fighter groups) in VIII.Fliegerkorps, flying the highly effective Bf 109F fighter, enjoyed a large tactical advantage over their Soviet VVS opponents. The VIII.Fliegerkorps also had over 200 Bf 109E7 and Bf 110 fighter-bombers, which could also acquit themselves well against Soviet fighters or be used to attack ground targets. Once the fighters cleared the airspace over the battlefield, VIII.Fliegerkorps' seven Stuka *Gruppen* were highly proficient in delivering precision attacks on enemy strongpoints, in order to support the advance of ground forces. Since 1939, the Luftwaffe had steadily improved its air–ground coordination system, and by 1942, German ground commanders could typically receive effective close air support within 15–20 minutes of a request. The Luftwaffe could also provide emergency aerial resupply to the Panzer spearheads, although Luftflotte 4 did not have a large force of Ju 52 transports at its disposal in June 1942.

The Wehrmacht's ability to mount successful ground offensives was heavily dependent upon the Luftwaffe being able to gain air superiority over the battlefield and to provide close air support. The Luftwaffe's Bf 109F fighter was not only an excellent air superiority platform but could also be employed as a fighter-bomber when necessary. Flown by some of the most experienced fighter pilots in the world, the Bf 109F was able to inflict grievous losses upon the Luftwaffe's VVS opponents. (Author's collection)

In addition to air support, the Luftwaffe also provided substantial ground combat support to the Ostheer. The 9.Flak-Division was attached to 6.Armee in *Blau*, and its Flak guns were highly effective in the dual-purpose role, either against enemy aircraft or tanks. In the open steppe terrain, the 8.8cm Flak gun was a particularly lethal anti-tank weapon, capable of destroying T-34 tanks out to a range of 2,000m.

Axis forces

At the start of *Blau*, the 200,000-man Hungarian Second Army was already at the front and ready to participate in the opening moves of the offensive. Colonel-General Vitéz Jány's Second Army consisted of nine light infantry divisions and one armoured division. However, only the three divisions in the Hungarian III Corps participated in the opening days of the offensive. Each light infantry division had six infantry battalions and two artillery battalions; the Hungarian divisions were particularly weak in terms of support weapons, with only 40 anti-tank guns (mostly 37mm) and 20 medium artillery pieces. The Hungarian 1st Armoured Division consisted of two tank, three motorized infantry, one reconnaissance and two motorized artillery battalions, with a total of over 150 armoured fighting vehicles (primarily the Panzer 38(t) and Toldi light tanks). In addition, the Second Army was supported by an aviation brigade with 14 Re 2000 fighters, 17 Ca 135 bombers and about a dozen reconnaissance aircraft.

The 227,000-man Italian Eighth Army, or Armata Italiana in Russia (ARMIR), was en route to the front at the start of *Blau* and not committed until the second week of the offensive. General Italo Gariboldi's Eighth Army consisted of five infantry divisions, three Alpine divisions, a cavalry division and two Blackshirt brigades. The 3rd Cavalry Division (PADA) was actually a hybrid motorized unit, with six battalions of Bersaglieri, three artillery battalions, a light tank battalion (with 61 L6/40 light tanks) and two squadrons of Semovente tank destroyers. Like the Hungarian infantry divisions, the Italian infantry and Alpine divisions each had six infantry

The Hungarian 1st Armoured Division started the campaign with a mix of Skoda Panzer 38(t) and 38M Toldi light tanks, which was based on the Swedish L-60 tank. The 8.5-ton Toldi was equipped with a 20mm anti-tank gun and had a maximum thickness of 13mm of armour, which meant it was poorly matched against most Soviet tanks. Instead, the Toldi was intended primarily for reconnaissance missions. Overall, the Toldi was slightly better than the German PzKpfw II light tank and the Soviet T-60. (Nik Cornish@www.stavka.org)

Hungarian troops of the Second Army move up to participate in the opening stages of *Blau*. The Hungarian infantry was lightly armed and equipped mostly with obsolete equipment, like their 8mm Mannlicher M1895 rifles. The state of training in the Hungarian Army was also low, which made its troops ill-suited to participating in a mobile campaign. (Nik Cornish@www.stavka.org)

battalions, but the Italians had somewhat better anti-tank, air defence and artillery support. Indeed, the Italian Eighth Army was fairly well equipped with artillery, boasting a total of 24 corps- and army-level artillery battalions, with nearly 300 artillery pieces. The Italian air contingent in ARMIR had four fighter squadrons, equipped with the MC 200 and MC 202 fighters, and a reconnaissance group.

Logistics

Unlike during *Barbarossa* or the German offensives of 1939–40, the Wehrmacht did not have a great deal of time to prepare the logistics for *Blau*, and it had to continue with ongoing combat operations that consumed fuel, ammunition and spare parts. Furthermore, the German logistic system in Russia had been jury rigged from the start, and nearly collapsed during the winter of 1941/42. Germany's reserves of aviation fuel and gasoline fell to dangerously low levels by January 1942 and units at the front were plagued by chronic fuel shortages. Heeresgruppe B

The Italian ARMIR had very little armoured support in July 1942. The 3rd Cavalry Division (PADA) had one battalion of Fiat L6/40 light tanks and some Semovente tank destroyers. The 6.8-ton L6/40 was armed with a 20mm cannon, and like the Hungarian Toldi, could not go toe-to-toe against Soviet tanks. (Nik Cornish@www.stavka.org)

established its main logistic base in Kharkov and had large supply dumps in Orel and Kursk, as well. Fuel stocks were adequate to support a limited duration, all-out attack, but once these were depleted, the mobility of the mechanized spearheads was dependent upon the regular arrival of fuel supply trains (*Betriebstoffzüge*) – each of which delivered about 400m^3 of fuel. The Ostheer measured fuel in terms of cubic metres (1m^3 = 1,000L) and calculated its fuel needs in terms of Verbrauchssatz (VS), with one VS being the amount of fuel needed to move a given unit's vehicles 100km. In June 1942, one VS for a typical *Panzer-Division* in 4.Panzer-Armee amounted to about 40m^3 of fuel (200,000L). Hoth's 4.Panzer-Armee started *Blau* with a total stockpile of 3,700 tons of fuel (about 5,000m^3), which was sufficient to provide each division with two VS of fuel on its vehicles and another three VS in corps-level fuel lagers. In addition, Heeresgruppe Süd provided each division with five days' worth of rations and hay for their horses, as well as one

basic load of ammunition. Some types of ammunition, such as heavy artillery ammunition and tungsten-core anti-tank rounds, were in short supply. A further complication was the difficulty of moving fuel and ammunition to fast-moving mechanized spearheads, due to the Ostheer's shortage of motor transport. The 4.Panzer-Armee was provided with three transport battalions, which had a total of about 300 trucks, but motor transport was in short supply. While the German *Eisenbahntruppen* could repair captured rail lines and facilities, the rail lines from Kharkov to Voronezh and Stalingrad were all single-track lines, which limited throughput. In a pinch, the Luftwaffe could deliver small amounts of fuel to forward units by Ju 52 transports (it took about 2.5 sorties to deliver 1m^3), but this was not a solution.

In addition to fuel shortages, the Ostheer was handicapped by the shortage of spare parts and the ability to repair damaged vehicles. Until 1942, the Wehrmacht had sent damaged vehicles back to Germany for repairs, but this system broke down in the winter of 1941/42. Expecting short campaigns, the Wehrmacht had not invested much effort in creating front-level maintenance units, but the failure of *Barbarossa* exposed the fallacy of this policy. Consequently, in early 1942, the OKH began to set up repair facilities in Russia, where vehicle maintenance could be conducted closer to the front. Krupp help set up one of the new K-Werke facilities in Dnepropetrovsk, which could repair up to 235 armoured vehicles per month. However, the shortage of basic items, such as tank road wheels, track pins and rubber tyres for trucks, limited the ability to return vehicles to front-line service in a timely manner. Many vehicles languished in the rear for weeks, awaiting parts.

SOVIET

At the start of *Blau*, the Bryansk and South-Western fronts had a combined total of just over 1 million personnel, although the actual number of combat troops was substantially less. In terms of organization, each front consisted of four field armies, each with four to eight rifle divisions and one to four tank brigades. A number of divisions and brigades were also retained under direct front control, in order to provide an operational reserve. Unlike the Germans, Stavka maintained a sizeable strategic reserve (Rezerv Verkhovnogo Glavnokomandovaniya, RVGK) around Moscow, including seven reserve armies with a total of 40 rifle divisions and 500 tanks, which could be used to reinforce the most critical sectors of the front.

Infantry
According to the *Shtatniy* (table of organization) of March 1942, a Soviet rifle division was supposed to have a total strength of 12,800 men, organized in three rifle regiments and an artillery regiment, plus support units. However, in late June 1942, most of the 28 rifle divisions in the South-Western Front and the 23 rifle divisions in the Bryansk Front were at about 60 per cent of their authorized strength. Like the Germans, the Soviet Union was having difficulty replacing the heavy losses of the last 12 months of combat. Even when near full strength, the Soviet rifle divisions lacked the firepower of their German opponents, and possessed far fewer veteran officers and NCOs, which limited their tactical capabilities. In late 1941, Stavka had begun

forming Guards rifle divisions from battle-proven infantry units; these units tended to be reinforced with additional personnel and equipment, which made them more resilient. However, of the 34 Guards rifle divisions available in June 1942, only three were in the South-Western Front and one in the Bryansk Front; nearly half were deployed against the Rzhev salient.

Soviet infantry tactics were simple, but effective, under the right conditions. Typically, Soviet rifle units were dogged in the defence, but given their limited anti-tank capabilities, they could hardly stand up to German mechanized units in open steppe terrain. In cities, forests and rough terrain, Soviet infantry were difficult to dislodge, and their logistical requirements were far more modest than German infantry units. On the other hand, Soviet infantry generally performed poorly in the attack in mid-1942, given their limited mobility and firepower. Infantry attacks tended to be unimaginative and poorly supported, leading to repeated failures. Given the high level of casualties and limited loyalty to the regime among non-Russian soldiers, it is not surprising that the Red Army suffered a steady drain of desertions, with many soldiers opting to surrender and serve as auxiliary personnel in the Wehrmacht (Hiwis).

A Soviet mortar crew moving into position. Both the Bryansk and South-Western fronts had established strong front-line positions after the failed offensive at Kharkov, but the open terrain west of Voronezh was not conducive to the defence. (Courtesy of the Central Museum of the Armed Forces, Moscow via Stavka)

Armour

Although the Red Army had a huge numerical advantage in armour, its tank units were not well organized and their tactical doctrine was still immature. The large collection of independent tank brigades and battalions allotted to the various fronts had nothing like the tactical effectiveness of the German *Panzer-Divisionen*. A typical independent Soviet tank brigade in June 1942 had about 40 tanks, half of which were T-60 or T-70 light tanks. Soviet armour had mostly been used in the infantry support role, rather than the deep penetration tactics employed by the enemy. In February 1942, Stavka decided to create 25 tank corps from existing and new armour units, with the first three forming in late March. The initial commitment of two of the new tank corps in the Battle of Kharkov in May was inauspicious – one

By mid-1942, the Soviets had refined the T-34 medium tank into an excellent design and cut its production time in half. With well-trained crews, the T-34 Model 1942 had the right mix of firepower and mobility to succeed on the battlefield. Unfortunately, Soviet armoured tactics were still fairly crude, and relied more on mass than manoeuvre – but this would change. (Nik Cornish@www.stavka.org)

was annihilated and the other was crippled. By the start of *Blau*, the Red Army had 22 tank corps and 98 separate tank brigades, of which 11 tanks corps and 22 tank brigades were assigned to the Bryansk and South-Western fronts. Altogether, these two fronts had 2,740 tanks or 30 per cent of the Red Army's tanks. Just after the end of the Battle of Kharkov, Stavka decided to form several tank armies from existing tank corps: the 3rd Tank Army was formed in the RVGK near Moscow, while the hastily formed 5th Tank Army was assigned to the Bryansk Front. On paper, the 5th Tank Army was a formidable force, with a total of 641 tanks, but it had negligible support units and had not trained together as a team. Nevertheless, Stavka envisioned the tank armies as an antidote to the German *Panzerarmee*, giving the Red Army a formation that could be used to counter-attack and defeat enemy pincer attacks – in theory.

At the tactical level, Soviet tank brigades did have some veteran crews and leaders by this point, but not enough yet to match German tactical prowess. The T-34 Model 1942 had slightly improved armoured protection and was an excellent medium tank, but its advantages were often nullified when it was committed into combat willy-nilly, with virtually untrained crews. Impressed by numbers, Stalin often urged Soviet commanders to commit their armour prematurely and en masse, with little infantry or artillery support. In contrast, German tankers habitually fought as part of a combined-arms team that included anti-tank units, artillery, motorized infantry, engineers and Flak guns. In the summer of 1942, the Red Army's tank forces were large, but fragile. The one saving grace was that Stavka kept one-quarter of its armour in reserve, enabling defeated units to be quickly restored.

Air support
The Soviet air armies in the south had suffered very heavy losses in the May–June fighting, and were at a low ebb when *Blau* began. By mid-1942, the VVS had replaced most of its older I-16 fighters with modern Yak-1 and

LaGG-3 fighters, but even these fighters were slightly slower and could not climb as fast as the Luftwaffe's Bf 109F-2. Altogether, the 2nd Air Army and 8th Air Army had a total of about 250 operational fighters at the start of *Blau*, with more than half being Yak-1s. These two air armies also had four regiments equipped with British-built Hurricane fighters, and one regiment with the American-built P-39 Airacobra. Aside from the technical shortcomings of Soviet fighters at this point in the war – which were often exacerbated by rushed production techniques – the Soviet fighter force was at a serious disadvantage against the Luftwaffe in terms of tactics and training. The *Jagdflieger* were trained as an offensive force, intended to conduct aggressive hunting patrols in enemy airspace, whereas Soviet fighter pilots were oriented towards defence of a given airspace. Furthermore, the VVS had not yet adopted the highly successful Finger-four (*Vierfingerschwarm*) formation used by the *Jagdflieger*. Yet the critical deficiency was in pilot training, with the VVS rushing novices into combat with minimal hours, only to be slaughtered by Luftwaffe *Experten*. General-major Khriukhin, commander of 8th Air Army, recognized the need for innovation in order to compete with the *Jagdflieger*, and one week after the beginning of *Blau*, he decided to form an elite fighter unit, which became the 9th Guards Fighter Aviation Regiment. This unit was assigned all the best fighter pilots from across 8th Air Army and was led by Major Lev Shestakov, one of the leading Soviet aces at that time.

In addition to its fighters, 2nd Air Army and 8th Air Army still retained substantial ground attack and bomber formations. While 2nd Air Army's ground attack regiments had been shredded by heavy losses, the two air armies could still field about 150 Il-2 Sturmoviks, which could be a serious threat to German motorized columns. Interestingly, 2nd Air Army and 8th Air Army had fewer than 100 operational Soviet-built Su-2 and Pe-2 bombers, but they had just received six regiments equipped with the American-built DB-7 (A-20) Boston medium bomber. The A-20s were well suited to long-range battlefield interdiction missions or raids on enemy airfields.

A group of Yak-1 fighters prepare for take-off. In mid-1942, the VVS was primarily equipped with the Yak-1 and LaGG-3 fighters, which were a vast improvement over the I-16s that opposed the Luftwaffe in 1941. Yet, aside from a few elite Guards regiments, the quality of Soviet aircrews was still quite poor, which led to very heavy losses against the Luftwaffe's *Experten*. Soviet fighters had better luck against German bombers, on the occasions when they could get past the escorting fighters. (Author's collection)

ORDER OF BATTLE, 28 JUNE 1942

RED ARMY

BRYANSK FRONT (GENERAL-LEYTENANT FILIPP I. GOLIKOV)

3rd Army (General-leytenant Pavel P. Korzun)
60th Rifle Division
137th Rifle Division
240th Rifle Division
269th Rifle Division
283rd Rifle Division
287th Rifle Division
104th Rifle Brigade
134th Rifle Brigade
79th Tank Brigade
150th Tank Brigade

13th Army (General-major Nikolai P. Pukhov)
15th Rifle Division
132nd Rifle Division
143rd Rifle Division
148th Rifle Division
307th Rifle Division
109th Rifle Brigade
129th Tank Brigade

40th Army (General-major Mikhail A. Parsegov)[2]
6th Rifle Division
45th Rifle Division
62nd Rifle Division
121st Rifle Division
160th Rifle Division
212th Rifle Division
111th Rifle Brigade
119th Rifle Brigade
141st Rifle Brigade
14th Tank Brigade (BT-7, Valentine)
170th Tank Brigade (25 tanks)

48th Army (General-major Grigoriy A. Khaliuzin)
6th Guards Rifle Division
8th Rifle Division
211th Rifle Division
280th Rifle Division
118th Rifle Brigade
122nd Rifle Brigade
55th Cavalry Division
80th Tank Brigade
202nd Tank Brigade

5th Tank Army (General-major Aleksandr I. Liziukov)[3]
2nd Tank Corps (General-major Andrei G. Kravchenko) (183 tanks total)
    26th Tank Brigade
    27th Tank Brigade
    148th Tank Brigade
11th Tank Corps (General-major Aleksei F. Popov) (191 tanks total)
    53rd Tank Brigade
    59th Tank Brigade
    160th Tank Brigade
19th Tank Brigade (65 tanks)

Front forces
1st Tank Corps (General-major Mikhail E. Katukov)
    1st Guards Tank Brigade
    49th Tank Brigade
    89th Tank Brigade
4th Tank Corps (General-major Vasily A. Mishulin) (179 tanks total)
    45th Tank Brigade
    47th Tank Brigade
    102nd Tank Brigade
16th Tank Corps (General-major Mikhail I. Pavelkin) (181 tanks)
    107th Tank Brigade
    109th Tank Brigade
    164th Tank Brigade
17th Tank Corps (General-major Nikolai V. Feklenko)[4] (145 tanks total)
    66th Tank Brigade
    67th Tank Brigade
    174th Tank Brigade
24th Tank Corps (General-major Vasily M. Badanov) (141 tanks total)
    4th Guards Tank Brigade
    54th Tank Brigade
    130th Tank Brigade
115th Tank Brigade
116th Tank Brigade
118th Tank Brigade
157th Tank Brigade
201st Tank Brigade
7th Cavalry Corps
    11th Cavalry Division
    17th Cavalry Division
    83rd Cavalry Division
8th Cavalry Corps
    21st Cavalry Division
    55th Cavalry Division
    112th Cavalry Division
1st Guards Rifle Division
284th Rifle Division
109th Rifle Brigade

2ND AIR ARMY (GENERAL-MAJOR STEPAN KRASOVSKIY)[5]

205th Fighter Aviation Division
    165th Fighter Aviation Regiment (13 x LaGG-3)
    563rd Fighter Aviation Regiment (3 x Yak-1)
    190th Ground Attack Aviation Regiment (14 x Il-2)
207th Fighter Aviation Division
    866th Fighter Aviation Regiment (15 x Yak-1)
    Unidentified fighter regiment (18 x LaGG-3)
266th Fighter Aviation Division
    15th Fighter Aviation Regiment (4 x LaGG-3)
    239th Fighter Aviation Regiment (13 x Yak-1)
    252nd Fighter Aviation Regiment (13 x Yak-1)
225th Ground Attack Aviation Division (27 x Il-2)
    825th Ground Attack Aviation Regiment
    872nd Ground Attack Aviation Regiment
227th Ground Attack Aviation Division (39 x Il-2)
    503rd Ground Attack Aviation Regiment
    525th Ground Attack Aviation Regiment
267th Ground Attack Aviation Division
    41st Ground Attack Aviation Regiment (11 x Il-2)
    683rd Ground Attack Aviation Regiment (11 x Il-2)
    874th Ground Attack Aviation Regiment (11 x Il-2)
223rd Bomber Aviation Division (46 x Pe-2)
    24th Bomber Aviation Regiment
    50th Bomber Aviation Regiment
    138th Bomber Aviation Regiment
244th Bomber Aviation Division (60 x A-20 Boston)
    45th Bomber Aviation Regiment

---

2   Replaced by General-leytenant Markian M. Popov on 3 July 1942.
3   Killed in action, 23 July 1942.
4   Relieved of command on 1 July 1942, replaced by General-major Ivan P. Korchagin.
5   Replaced by Polkovnik Konstantin N. Smirnov on 4 July 1942.

449th Bomber Aviation Regiment
861st Bomber Aviation Regiment
208th Night-Bomber Aviation Division (36 x R-5, 20 other aircraft)
    620th Night-Bomber Aviation Regiment
    646th Night-Bomber Aviation Regiment
    715th Night-Bomber Aviation Regiment
    719th Night-Bomber Aviation Regiment
17th Fighter Aviation Regiment (40 x P-39)

SOUTH-WESTERN FRONT (MARSHAL SEMYON K. TIMOSHENKO)

9th Army (General-major Feofan A. Parkhomenko)
51st Rifle Division
81st Rifle Division
106th Rifle Division
140th Rifle Division
255th Rifle Division
296th Rifle Division
318th Rifle Division
333rd Rifle Division
12th Tank Brigade
5th Cavalry Corps
    30th Cavalry Division
    34th Cavalry Division
    60th Cavalry Division
21st Army (General-major Aleksei I. Danilov)
76th Rifle Division
227th Rifle Division
293rd Rifle Division
297th Rifle Division
301st Rifle Division
8th NKVD Motorized Rifle Division
13th Tank Corps (General-major Petr E. Shurov)[6] (163 tanks total)
    85th Tank Brigade
    167th Tank Brigade
10th Tank Brigade (38 tanks)
28th Army (General-leytenant Dmitri I. Riabyshev)
13th Guards Rifle Division
38th Rifle Division
169th Rifle Division
175th Rifle Division
226th Rifle Division
244th Rifle Division
300th Rifle Division
23rd Tank Corps (General-major Abram M. Khasin) (128 tanks total)
    6th Guards Tank Brigade
    91st Tank Brigade
    114th Tank Brigade
65th Tank Brigade (c. 45 tanks)
90th Tank Brigade (c. 45 tanks)
38th Army (General-major Kirill S. Moskalenko)
81st Rifle Division
124th Rifle Division
162nd Rifle Division
199th Rifle Division
242nd Rifle Division
277th Rifle Division
278th Rifle Division
304th Rifle Division
22nd Tank Corps (General-major Aleksandr A. Shamshin) (49 tanks total)
    3rd Tank Brigade
    13th Tank Brigade
    36th Tank Brigade
133rd Tank Brigade
156th Tank Brigade
159th Tank Brigade

168th Tank Brigade
One independent tank battalion (OTB) (94 tanks total)
Front forces
14th Tank Corps (General-major Nikolai N. Radkevich)
    138th Tank Brigade
    139th Tank Brigade
57th Tank Brigade
58th Tank Brigade
84th Tank Brigade
88th Tank Brigade
158th Tank Brigade
176th Tank Brigade
Two independent tank battalions (OTBs)
3rd Guards Cavalry Corps
    5th Guards Cavalry Division
    6th Guards Cavalry Division
    32nd Cavalry Division

8TH AIR ARMY (GENERAL-MAJOR TIMOFEI T. KHRIUKHIN)

206th Fight Aviation Division
    427th Fighter Aviation Regiment (Yak-1)
    515th Fighter Aviation Regiment (Yak-1)
    876th Fighter Aviation Regiment (Yak-1)
    31st Fighter Aviation Regiment (LaGG-3)
220th Fighter Aviation Division
    9th Guards Fighter Aviation Regiment (Yak-1)
    248th Fighter Aviation Regiment (Yak-1)
    296th Fighter Aviation Regiment (Yak-1)
    2nd Fighter Aviation Regiment (LaGG-3)
235th Fighter Aviation Division
    46th Fighter Aviation Regiment (Hurricane)
    180th Fighter Aviation Regiment (Hurricane)
    191st Fighter Aviation Regiment (Hurricane)
    436th Fighter Aviation Regiment (Hurricane)
268th Fighter Aviation Division
    273rd Fighter Aviation Regiment (Yak-1)
    875th Fighter Aviation Regiment (Yak-1)
    512th Fighter Aviation Regiment (LaGG-3)
269th Fighter Aviation Division
    6th Fighter Aviation Regiment (Yak-1)
    148th Fighter Aviation Regiment (Yak-1)
    254th Fighter Aviation Regiment (LaGG-3)
226th Ground Attack Aviation Division
    504th Ground Attack Aviation Regiment (Il-2)
    505th Ground Attack Aviation Regiment (Il-2)
228th Ground Attack Aviation Division
    211th Ground Attack Aviation Regiment (Il-2)
    285th Ground Attack Aviation Regiment (Il-2)
    431st Ground Attack Aviation Regiment (Il-2)
221st Bomber Aviation Division
    57th Bomber Aviation Regiment (A-20 Boston)
    745th Bomber Aviation Regiment (A-20 Boston)
    794th Bomber Aviation Regiment (A-20 Boston)
270th Bomber Aviation Division
    52nd Bomber Aviation Regiment (Su-2)
    135th Bomber Aviation Regiment (Su-2)
    826th Bomber Aviation Regiment (Su-2)
    94th Bomber Aviation Regiment (Pe-2)
271st Night-Bomber Aviation Division
    10th Bomber Aviation Regiment (SB, Il-4, Pe-2, R-5)
    626th Bomber Aviation Regiment (SB, Il-4, Pe-2, R-5)
272nd Night-Bomber Aviation Division
    596th Night-Bomber Aviation Regiment (U-2)
    709th Night-Bomber Aviation Regiment (U-2)
    714th Night-Bomber Aviation Regiment (U-2)
434th Fighter Aviation Regiment (Yak-1)
13th Bomber Aviation Regiment (Pe-2)
8th Independent Reconnaissance Aviation Regiment (ORAP)

---

6   Died of wounds, 2 July 1942.

REINFORCEMENTS

4 July 1942
18th Tank Corps (181 tanks)
5 July 1942
1st Fighter Aviation Army (231 fighters)
8 July 1942
60th Army (General-leytenant Maksim A. Antoniuk)
10 July 1942
25th Tank Corps (General-major Petr R. Pavlov) (159 tanks)
(7th Reserve Army) 62nd Army (General-major Vladimir Ia. Kolpakchi)[7]
    33rd Guards Rifle Division
    147th Rifle Division
    181st Rifle Division
    184th Rifle Division
    192nd Rifle Division
    196th Rifle Division
(5th Reserve Army) 63rd Army (General-leytenant Vasily I. Kuznetsov)
    14th Guards Rifle Division
    1st Rifle Division
    127th Rifle Division
    153rd Rifle Division
    197th Rifle Division
    203rd Rifle Division
(1st Reserve Army) 64th Army (General-leytenant Vasily I. Chuikov)
    29th Rifle Division
    112nd Rifle Division
    214th Rifle Division
    229th Rifle Division
    66th Naval Rifle Brigade
    154th Naval Rifle Brigade
    137th Tank Brigade (35 tanks)
26 July 1942
1st Tank Army (General-major Kirill S. Moskalenko)
    13th Tank Corps (General-major Trofim I. Tanaschishin)
    28th Tank Corps (General-major Georgy S. Rodin)
    158th Heavy Tank Brigade (KV-1)
    131st Rifle Division
    399th Rifle Division
4th Tank Army (General-major Vasily D. Kriuchenkin)
    22nd Tank Corps (General-major Aleksandr A. Shamshin)
    23rd Tank Corps (General-major Abram M. Khasin)
    133rd Tank Brigade

WEHRMACHT

HEERESGRUPPE SÜD (GENERALFELDMARSCHALL FEDOR VON BOCK)

2.Armee (Generaloberst Maximilian von Weichs)
LV.Armee-Korps (Generalmajor Rudolf Freiherr von Roman)
    45.Infanterie-Division
    95.Infanterie-Division
      Sturmgeschütz-Abteilung 243
    299.Infanterie-Division
    1.SS-Infanterie-Brigade (mot.)
Under 2.Armee control:
    88.Infanterie-Division
    383.Infanterie-Division

4.Panzer-Armee (Generaloberst Hermann Hoth)
XXIV.Panzer-Korps (General der Panzertruppen Wilibald Freiherr von Langermann und Erlenkamp)[8]
    9.Panzer-Division (Generalleutnant Johannes Baessler)
    11.Panzer-Division (General der Panzertruppen Hermann Balck)
    3.Infanterie-Division (mot.) (Generalmajor Helmuth Schlömer)
XXXXVIII.Panzer-Korps (General der Panzertruppen Werner Kempf)
    24.Panzer-Division (Generalleutnant Bruno Ritter von Hauenschild)
    16.Infanterie-Division (mot.) (Generalleutnant Sigfrid Henrici)
    Infanterie-Division Grossdeutschland (mot.) (Generalleutnant Walter Hörnlein)
      Sturmgeschütz-Abteilung 226
XIII.Armee-Korps (General der Infanterie Erich Straube)
    82.Infanterie-Division (Generalleutnant Friedrich Hossbach)
    385.Infanterie-Division (Generalleutnant Karl Eibl)
Hungarian Second Army (Colonel-General Vitéz Gusztáv Jány)
III Corps (Brigadier-General György Rakovszky)
    6th Light Infantry Division
    7th Light Infantry Division
    9th Light Infantry Division
VII.Armee-Korps (General der Artillerie Ernst-Eberhard Hell)
    387.Infanterie-Division
6.Armee (General der Panzertruppe Friedrich Paulus)
XXXX.Panzer-Korps (General der Kavallerie Georg Stumme)
    3.Panzer-Division (Generalleutnant Hermann Breith)
    23.Panzer-Division (Generalleutnant Hans Freiherr von Boineburg-Lengsfeld)[9]
      Sturmgeschütz-Abteilung 201
    29.Infanterie-Division (mot.) (Generalmajor Max Fremerey)
    100.Jäger-Division
    336.Infanterie-Division
LI.Armee-Korps (General der Artillerie Walter von Seydlitz-Kurzbach)
    44.Infanterie-Division
    62.Infanterie-Division
    71.Infanterie-Division
    297.Infanterie-Division
VIII.Armee-Korps (General der Artillerie Walter Heitz)
    305.Infanterie-Division
    389.Infanterie-Division
XVII.Armee-Korps (General der Infanterie Karl Hollidt)
    79.Infanterie-Division
    113.Infanterie-Division
      Sturmgeschütz-Abteilung 244
    294.Infanterie-Division
XXIX.Armee-Korps (General der Infanterie Hans von Obstfelder)
    57.Infanterie-Division
    75.Infanterie-Division
    168.Infanterie-Division
      Sturmgeschütz-Abteilung 177
    376.Infanterie-Division
Under Heeresgruppe Süd control:
9.Flak-Division (Oberst Wolfgang Pickert)
    Flak-Regiment 12
    Flak-Regiment 37
    Flak-Regiment 91
    Flak-Regiment 104

---

7 Formerly the 7th Reserve Army. General-leytenant Vasily I. Chuikov assumed command on 10 September 1942.

8 Killed in action, 3 October 1942.

9 Relieved of command 20 July 1942, reinstated in August. Wounded in action, 27 December 1942.

Operational tanks, 28 June 1942

Unit	PzKpfw II	PzKpfw III (short)	PzKpfw III (long)	PzKpfw IV (short)	PzKpfw IV (long)	Pz-befehlswagen	Total
9.Panzer-Division	22	38	61	9	12	2	**144**
11.Panzer-Division	15	14	110	1	12	3	**155**
3.Infanterie-Division (mot.)	10		35		8	1	**54**
24.Panzer-Division	32	54	56	20	12	7	**181**
16.Infanterie-Division (mot.)	10		35		8	1	**54**
Infanterie-Division Grossdeutschland	12	2		18	12	1	**45**
3.Panzer-Division	25	66	40	21	12		**164**
23.Panzer-Division	27	50	34	17	10		**138**
29.Infanterie-Division (mot.)	12		36		8		**56**
Total	**165**	**224**	**407**	**86**	**94**	**15**	**991**

Luftflotte 4 (Generaloberst Alexander Löhr)[10]
IV.Fliegerkorps (General der Flieger Kurt Pflugbeil)
    Stab, I., II., III./Kampfgeschwader 27 (76 x He 111H)
    Stab, I., II., III./Kampfgeschwader 51 (54 x Ju 88A)
    II./Kampfgeschwader 54 (13 x Ju 88)
    Stab, I., II., III./Kampfgeschwader 55 (79 x He 111H)
    Stab, I., II., III./Kampfgeschwader 76 (56 x Ju 88A)
    Stab, I./Kampfgeschwader 77 (12 x Ju 88A)
VIII.Fliegerkorps (Generaloberst Wolfram Freiherr von Richthofen)
    Stab, I./Kampfgeschwader 100 (29 x He 111H)
    II./Sturzkampfgeschwader 1 (44 x Ju 87)
    Stab, I., II., III./Sturzkampfgeschwader 2 (83 x Ju 87)
    Stab, I., II., III./Sturzkampfgeschwader 77 (71 x Ju 87)
    Stab, I., II./Schlachtgeschwader 1 (42 x Bf 109E7, 35 x Hs 129B, 12 x Hs 123)
    Stab, I., II., III./Zerstörergeschwader 1 (17 x Bf 109E7, 58 x Bf 110D/E/F)
    Stab, I., II., III./Zerstörergeschwader 2 (23 x Bf 109E7, 63 x Bf 110D/E/F)
    Stab, I., II., III./Jagdgeschwader 3 (72 x Bf 109F)
    Stab, I., II., III., 15./Jagdgeschwader 52 (71 x Bf 109F)
    I./Jagdgeschwader 53 (33 x Bf 109F)
    Stab, II./Jagdgeschwader 77 (23 x Bf 109F)

Operational aircraft, 28 June 1942

Type	Model	Number of serviceable aircraft
Fighters	Bf 109F	199
Fighter-bombers	Bf 109E7	82
	Bf 110D/E/F	121
Bombers	He 111H	184
	Ju 88A	135
Ground attack	Ju 87	198
	Hs 129B	35
	Hs 123	12
Long-range reconnaissance	Ju 88D, Do 17	45
Tactical reconnaissance	Fw 189	100
	Bf 110	16
	Hs 126	29
Total		**1,156**

Reinforcements:
10 July 1942
323.Infanterie-Division (from France), assigned to 2.Armee
384.Infanterie-Division (from 1.Panzer-Armee), assigned to 6.Armee

21–25 July 1942: remainder of Hungarian Second Army
Hungarian IV Corps (Colonel-General Lajos Csatay)
    10th Light Infantry Division
    12th Light Infantry Division
    13th Light Infantry Division
Hungarian VII Corps (Major-General Ernö Gyimesi)
    19th Light Infantry Division
    20th Light Infantry Division
    23rd Light Infantry Division
1st Armoured Field Division
2nd Aviation Brigade
    1/1, 2/1 Fighter squadrons (total of 22 x Re 2000)
    4/1 Bomber Squadron (14 x Ca 135)
    3/1 Reconnaissance Squadron (4 x He 111P, 12 x He 46)
22 July 1942: transferred from 1.Panzer-Armee
XIV.Panzer-Korps (General der Infanterie Gustav von Wietersheim)
    16.Panzer-Division (Generalleutnant Hans-Valentin Hube)
    60.Infanterie-Division (mot.) (Generalleutnant Otto Kohlermann)
30 July 1942: assigned to 4.Panzer-Armee
Romanian VI Corps (Lieutenant-General Corneliu Draglina)
    1st Infantry Division
    2nd Infantry Division
    4th Infantry Division
    20th Infantry Division
8 August 1942
22.Panzer-Division (Generalleutnant Wilhelm von Apell)
11–15 August 1942
Italian Eighth Army (General Italo Gariboldi)
    Italian II Corps (General Giovanni Zanghieri)
        2nd Infantry Division Sforzesca
        3rd Infantry Division Ravenna
        5th Infantry Division Cosseria
        23rd CCNN Brigade Marzo
    Italian XXXV Corps (General Giovanni Messe)
        9th Infantry Division Pasubio
        52nd Infantry Division Torino
        3rd Cavalry Division Principe Amedeo Duca d'Aosta
        3rd CCNN Brigade Gennaio
    Italian Alpini Corps (General Gabriele Nasci)
        2nd Alpine Division Tridentina
        3rd Alpine Division Julia
        4th Alpine Division Cuneense
    Barbo Cavalry Brigade
    Corpo Italiano di Spedizione
        21st Group Caccia Terrestre (50 x MC 200/202 fighters)
        71st Group Osservazione Aerea (20 x Ca 311 reconnaissance)

10 Replaced by Generaloberst Wolfram Freiherr von Richthofen on 4 July 1942.

OPPOSING PLANS

GERMAN

As the winter snows faded in Russia, Hitler began to consider his next strategic move. German options were shaped by the blunt fact that the Wehrmacht's offensive capacity had been seriously eroded by ten months of continuous combat and losses. At his Wolfsschanze headquarters in East Prussia, Hitler was informed by Generaloberst Franz Halder, chief of the OKH, that between 1 October 1941 and 15 March 1942, the Ostheer had lost 74,183 vehicles and 179,609 horses, but received only 7,441 vehicles and 20,000 horses as replacements; in short, German tactical mobility would be significantly reduced. Likewise, Halder pointed out that manpower losses had greatly exceeded replacements, and by spring 1942, the Ostheer was short 625,000 men – the equivalent of over 30 divisions. Although new conscripts could be trained in a few months, the heavy losses of junior officers and non-commissioned officers would take far longer to rectify, which had a negative impact on tactical efficiency at the platoon/company level. Similarly, the Luftwaffe formations deployed in Russia in 1942 had 30 per cent fewer aircraft than they had for *Barbarossa*, in part due to losses and in part due to greater commitments in Western Europe and North Africa. As a result of these facts, which Hitler accepted, the Wehrmacht was no longer capable of mounting another all-out effort like *Barbarossa*. At best, the Ostheer could only mount major operations on a select portion of the Eastern Front.

Halder and his chief of operations, Generalmajor Adolf Heusinger, argued that the Ostheer should remain on the defensive during 1942 and focus on rebuilding its strength. Only limited operations should be conducted, to clean up areas like the Crimea. Halder and Heusinger claimed that the Ostheer would be able to repulse any enemy offensives in 1942, while building up for a knockout blow in 1943. However, the OKH recommendations were overly conservative, and Hitler was by nature a risk-taker. He recognized that he needed to achieve a decisive victory in Russia before the Anglo-Americans could mount a serious effort in the West, or Germany would permanently lose the strategic initiative. Hitler also rightly pointed out that if the Ostheer spent 1942 refitting, then the Red Army would also benefit from the lull to replace its own losses and become an even tougher opponent in 1943. No, the Third Reich had to strike while decisive victory was still possible. Yet the key question was: Where could Germany employ its limited resources with the best chance of achieving a major success in Russia? Furthermore,

Operational intentions on the Eastern Front, summer 1942

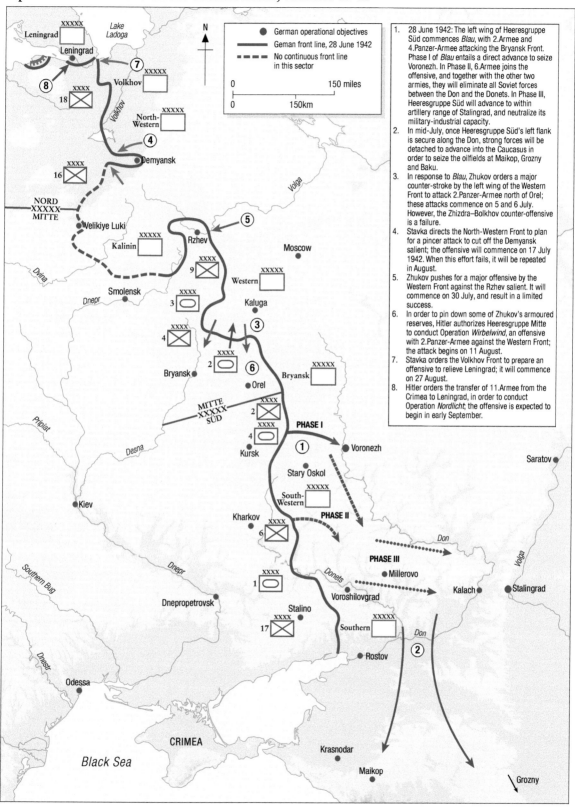

Legend:
- ● German operational objectives
- ── Geman front line, 28 June 1942
- - - - No continuous front line in this sector

0 ——— 150 miles
0 ——— 150km

1. 28 June 1942: The left wing of Heeresgruppe Süd commences *Blau*, with 2.Armee and 4.Panzer-Armee attacking the Bryansk Front. Phase I of *Blau* entails a direct advance to seize Voronezh. In Phase II, 6.Armee joins the offensive, and together with the other two armies, they will eliminate all Soviet forces between the Don and the Donets. In Phase III, Heeresgruppe Süd will advance to within artillery range of Stalingrad, and neutralize its military-industrial capacity.
2. In mid-July, once Heeresgruppe Süd's left flank is secure along the Don, strong forces will be detached to advance into the Caucasus in order to seize the oilfields at Maikop, Grozny and Baku.
3. In response to *Blau*, Zhukov orders a major counter-stroke by the left wing of the Western Front to attack 2.Panzer-Armee north of Orel; these attacks commence on 5 and 6 July. However, the Zhizdra–Bolkhov counter-offensive is a failure.
4. Stavka directs the North-Western Front to plan for a pincer attack to cut off the Demyansk salient; the offensive will commence on 17 July 1942. When this effort fails, it will be repeated in August.
5. Zhukov pushes for a major offensive by the Western Front against the Rzhev salient. It will commence on 30 July, and result in a limited success.
6. In order to pin down some of Zhukov's armoured reserves, Hitler authorizes Heeresgruppe Mitte to conduct Operation *Wirbelwind*, an offensive with 2.Panzer-Armee against the Western Front; the attack begins on 11 August.
7. Stavka orders the Volkhov Front to prepare an offensive to relieve Leningrad; it will commence on 27 August.
8. Hitler orders the transfer of 11.Armee from the Crimea to Leningrad, in order to conduct Operation *Nordlicht*; the offensive is expected to begin in early September.

should the Wehrmacht focus on destroying the main Soviet field armies, or on seizing key territorial objectives?

Hitler was confronted with a variety of opinions about where the next summer offensive should be conducted. Generalfeldmarschall Georg Wilhelm von Küchler, commander of Heeresgruppe Nord, argued that a major offensive should be mounted in the north, to capture Leningrad and complete a ground link-up with Finnish forces. There was no doubt that Leningrad was a key objective and its loss would be a serious blow to Soviet morale, but the Red Army's overall offensive capacity would not be crippled. Generalfeldmarschall Günther von Kluge, commander of Heeresgruppe Mitte, was mostly concerned that the Soviets would launch a major effort to cut off the 9.Armee in the vulnerable Rzhev salient; they had nearly succeeded in the winter, and von Kluge expected a much more powerful enemy offensive in the summer. In order to reduce the enemy pressure on his front, von Kluge advocated a pincer operation to eliminate the Sukhinichi salient, which would help reduce the threat to the Rzhev salient. Subsequently, von Kluge recommended a follow-up offensive by 2.Panzer-Armee, due north from the Bolkhov–Orel region, to destroy enemy reserves gathering around Moscow. Clearly, the enemy would have to fight to defend its capital and the Wehrmacht could be expected to inflict heavy losses, even if Moscow did not fall. Hitler listened to these proposals, but believed that, at best, they could only deliver ordinary victories, without significantly enhancing Germany's strategic situation. Nevertheless, he did not actually reject any of these ideas out of hand.

Generalfeldmarschall Hermann Göring, head of the Luftwaffe, was instrumental in making the case to Hitler that oil was the key to strategic success. Göring argued that Germany needed access to oil to guarantee victory in a mechanized war, and 70 per cent of the Soviet Union's oil reserves were located in the Caucasus; ergo, a German offensive to seize the Caucasus would both gain oil for the Wehrmacht while denying it to its enemy. Deprived of the majority of its oil reserves, the Red Army would be permanently weakened. Furthermore, the Red Army forces protecting the Caucasus were assessed to be less capable than those protecting Leningrad or Moscow, so the region could be seized in the kind of rapid manoeuvre campaign in which the Wehrmacht excelled. Hitler liked this rationale because it meant that it might be possible to quickly achieve a strategic victory at relatively low cost. Consequently, on 5 April 1942, he issued Führer Directive No. 41, which stated that the overall objective of the summer offensive was to 'destroy the enemy before the Don, in order to secure the Caucasus oilfields'. Hitler told his senior commanders that, 'if I do not get the oil of Maikop and Grozny, then I must end this war.'

Hitler discussing plans for the upcoming summer offensive with his commanders. Note von Weichs, Paulus and von Bock on the Führer's left. Hitler's primary strategic rationale for *Blau* was the capture of the Soviet oilfields, but he also wanted to finish off the Soviet Union before the Anglo-Americans could create a second front in the West. (Author's collection)

The offensive, originally referred to as *Siegfried* but then changed to *Blau*, was conceived as a multi-phased operation, consisting of consecutive offensive pulses, each synchronized to bring the maximum force to bear at the key place and time. The main effort would be made by Heeresgruppe Süd, while the other two army groups remained on the defensive. However, rather than choose between prioritizing the destruction of enemy forces or seizing terrain objectives, Hitler ensured that *Blau* was designed to simultaneously accomplish both tasks. The bulk of Soviet field armies west of the Don were to be encircled and destroyed in a series of hard-hitting mobile battles reminiscent of the early days of *Barbarossa*. Subsequently, Hitler specified that the city of Voronezh must be taken, along with crossings over the Don, before the army group moved into the Caucasus to seize the oilfields. However, Hitler regarded the advance towards Stalingrad as merely a flank-guard for the main effort into the Caucasus, and Führer Directive No. 41 was vague about the importance of capturing the city. Instead, Hitler stated that it would be sufficient if 'the city was brought under fire from heavy artillery so that it may no longer be of any use as an industrial or communications centre'.

Phase I of *Blau* would begin on the left wing of Heeresgruppe Süd, with 4.Panzer-Armee tearing a hole in the boundary between the Bryansk and South-Western fronts. Then, 6.Armee would join in and expand this gap, enabling a strike east to seize Voronezh. Once Voronezh was taken, the second phase would begin with the left wing of Heeresgruppe Süd wheeling to the south-east, a move intended to envelop Soviet forces deployed between the Donets and the Don with a great pincer movement to link up with 1.Panzer-Armee. Following the elimination of the main Soviet field armies west of the Don, the third phase would consist of Heeresgruppe Süd advancing across the Don, the left wing advancing towards Stalingrad while the right wing pushed into the Caucasus. The Italian and Hungarian armies were merely expected to hold the line on the Don, while the German mechanized spearheads raced forwards to seize their objectives. The OKH believed that the primary objectives of *Blau* could be achieved in about six weeks, although it was recognized that mop-up operations in the Caucasus might continue for some time. Once *Blau* was completed, Hitler wanted as much of the strike force refitted and made fully operational again as soon as possible.

In order to be able to conduct an offensive on the scale of *Blau*, the Wehrmacht had to concentrate its resources in Heeresgruppe Süd, while taking resources from the other two army groups. During spring 1942, the lion's share of German replacement personnel and equipment went to von Bock's Heeresgruppe Süd, which left the other two army groups in a threadbare state. Hitler also turned to Mussolini to gain a greater Italian troop commitment on the Eastern Front, as well as to the Hungarians and the Romanians. Mussolini felt that Italy was already making a strong commitment in North Africa and the Balkans, but provided the Italian Eighth Army for *Blau*. Altogether, over 600,000 Axis troops would participate in *Blau*, making up for the shortage of German units. Neither Mussolini nor the other Axis heads of state were brought into the planning of *Blau* due to concerns that they could not be fully trusted to safeguard the details.

Blau, as written by Generalmajor Heusinger's staff at the OKH, was based upon a number of assumptions. First, the OKH's intelligence arm assessed that the Red Army's strategic reserves were significantly smaller than their actual strength, and were located around Moscow. While the Red Army's main strength was indeed positioned in the centre, the OKH believed that Stalin would not be able to replace heavy losses in the south in a timely manner. The OKH's Abwehr (military intelligence) erroneously assessed Soviet armour production as 600–700 tanks per month, but the actual figure was over 2,200. Second, the OKH expected the Soviet forces in the southern theatre to stand and fight in the open as they had in 1941, enabling the Wehrmacht's mechanized pincers to surround large hauls of prisoners. Third, while recognizing the lower combat effectiveness of the Axis satellite troops, the OKH assumed that they would at least be capable of holding ground gained by von Bock's mechanized spearheads and protecting the flanks of the German vanguard. Finally, the OKH assumed that Heeresgruppe Süd could attain all its objectives with the forces available in a short campaign that ended well before winter. Many of these planning assumptions for *Blau* were quite dangerous, but they were not recognized as such at the time.

In order to deceive the Soviets about *Blau*'s true objectives, the OKH developed a deception plan known as *Fall Kreml* (*Kremlin*). Von Klüge's Heeresgruppe Mitte was ordered to conduct activities which suggested that the main German summer offensive would be aimed at Moscow. Von Kluge used preparations for an attack on the Sukhinichi salient to simulate a much larger operation, with 2.Panzer-Armee spearheading an attack from the Bolkhov region. The Luftwaffe also increased reconnaissance activity over the Moscow region, to suggest an impending offensive.

Meanwhile, Heeresgruppe Süd had to fend off the impending Soviet offensive at Kharkov and complete the conquest of the Crimea before *Blau* could begin. Von Bock's staff developed the *Fridericus* plan to deal with Timoshenko's offensive, while Generaloberst Erich von Manstein's 11.Armee in the Crimea developed Operation *Trappenjagd* (*Bustard Hunt*) to crush the Soviet forces in the Kerch Peninsula. After *Trappenjagd*, von Manstein would complete the siege of Sevastopol, thereby eliminating the last Soviet position in the Crimea. Once the Crimea was occupied, von Manstein's 11.Armee would be available for commitment elsewhere, but Hitler remained undecided about its follow-on mission. The OKH wanted to keep 11.Armee as a strategic reserve in the south, or to use it in the Caucasus to reinforce the push for the oilfields, but Hitler would not commit to either role. Incredibly, Hitler decided to keep open the idea of conducting an autumn offensive at Leningrad, while also promising von Kluge that he would obtain some forces to conduct a spoiling offensive against the Soviet Western Front.

It is also important to remember that Generaloberst Erwin Rommel's Panzer-Armee Afrika was simultaneously conducting a major offensive in North Africa and competing for resources with the Ostheer. By spring 1942, the OKH had already sent over 700 tanks to North Africa, and after the Battle of Gazala, which ended just a week before *Blau* began, Rommel demanded more tanks and fuel to replace his losses so he could advance into Egypt. Hitler should have put a break upon Rommel, since an offensive into Egypt would divert resources from the more critical Eastern Front, but he did not. Rommel's offensive was just enough to deprive the Ostheer of critical resources that could have reinforced the main effort and provided an operational buffer if anything went wrong.

While *Blau* has been much criticized by historians, the original plan did make good use of the principles of war, particularly surprise, mass and manoeuvre. The Wehrmacht did have the resources to reach Voronezh, Stalingrad and at least some of the oilfields in the Caucasus, although it was unclear if achieving these goals would actually cripple the Soviet Union's military-industrial base. *Blau* was a high-risk plan, but it could work if everything went well and there were no unexpected surprises. However,

One of the objectives of *Blau* was to eliminate Soviet armaments production in Stalingrad, particularly the Tractor Factory (StZ), which had been converted to manufacture T-34 tanks. By July 1942, StZ was building up to 421 T-34 tanks per month, or about 13 per day. Nearly one-third of T-34s were being manufactured in Stalingrad, and destruction of StZ would impinge upon the Red Army's ability to replace armoured losses, at least temporarily. (Author's collection)

Hitler's predilection for micromanagement was at its worst during the execution of *Blau*, with the Führer constantly shifting operational priorities and sub-unit missions. Instead of focusing on one goal and ruthlessly carrying it through to successful completion, Hitler wanted to pursue a variety of near-simultaneous objectives, which tended to stretch German resources to breaking point.

SOVIET

In contrast to the frequent criticisms of *Blau*, few historians have bothered to mention that the Soviet Stavka had no real plan for winning the war at this stage. In late March 1942, the Soviet State Defence Committee (Gosudarstvennyj Komitet Oborony, GKO) held a conference in Moscow to discuss military strategy for the rest of 1942. Marshal Boris M. Shaposhnikov, chief of the General Staff, argued that since the Red Army and Soviet industry were still recovering from the heavy losses of 1941–42, the best course was to adopt a policy of 'active defence' until conditions improved. Under this strategy, the Red Army would conduct local offensives in sectors where it had an advantage, in order to keep the enemy off balance and inflict losses. Most of the participants agreed with this concept, with Timoshenko recommending an offensive to retake Kharkov, while others suggested Leningrad, Demyansk and the Crimea. Zhukov was the most vociferous, arguing forcefully for a full-scale pincer attack against the Rzhev salient. However, Stalin was not impressed by any of these suggestions, which he regarded as 'half-measures' that would not contribute much to final victory. Stalin, like Hitler, did not reject outright any of these recommended options, but rather he approved Timoshenko's Kharkov offensive and deferred on the others.

The primary factor driving the formulation of Soviet strategy in early 1942 was apprehension about the next German summer offensive. While the Soviet armaments industry was beginning to recover and ramp up production of tanks, aircraft and artillery, the field armies were still seriously short of equipment. Even worse, the senior leadership was worried about the shaky state of front-line morale and the shortage of trained junior leaders. Although some historians have suggested that the Russo-German War was decided by the failure of *Barbarossa* in 1941, this was not apparent to Stalin and the rest of the GKO, who were still far from certain of eventual victory. Stavka assessed that the most likely German course of action would be to conduct a full-scale attack against the Bryansk Front, in order to approach Moscow from the south. Consequently, Stalin ordered that the majority of armour in Stavka's RVGK reserve should be deployed behind the Bryansk Front, with the remainder kept around Moscow. Only once German intentions were clear would he allow the armoured reserves to be committed in a counter-offensive to stop the enemy advance.

However, the German victories at Kharkov and Kerch in May 1942 sent a jolt through Stavka, which saw the enemy smash its local offensives with ridiculous ease. Clearly, the Germans had recovered some of their operational-level effectiveness, while Soviet operations had been poorly coordinated fiascoes. As a result of these defeats, Stavka became less willing to take large operational risks and demanded greater control over future operations, which Stalin approved. Although the Volkhov, North-West, Kalinin and Western fronts were all working on offensive plans which they expected to execute during the summer of 1942, Stavka temporarily delayed any major offensive operations until the enemy's intentions became apparent.

By the fortunes of war, an incident occurred on 19 June which revealed the German intentions. A German Fieseler Storch liaison plane carrying Major Joachim Reichel, the operations officer for 23.Panzer-Division, was shot down near the front. Reichel was killed and Soviet troops recovered his maps, which included notes about the initial objectives of the upcoming German offensive. Although incomplete, Reichel's documents revealed that the Germans intended to make their main effort in the south, not against Moscow. Timoshenko duly forwarded the captured documents to Stavka, but Stalin regarded them as fakes and an effort by the Germans to entice the Red Army to move its reserves away from the capital. Consequently, the intelligence windfall led to no major adjustment of Soviet defensive plans. On the other side, Hitler was convinced that the plans for *Blau* were compromised and that the offensive should begin as soon as possible.

By mid-1942, Soviet strategy was developed by General Georgy Zhukov and the General Staff, but dictator Josef Stalin had the final say. Although first among equals in the General Staff, Zhukov was still commander of the Western Front and he pressed for resources to be prioritized to his sector of the front. Combined with Stalin's lingering fear that the Germans would make another attempt to capture Moscow in 1942, Stavka did not expect the Germans to make their main effort in southern Russia. (Author's collection)

THE CAMPAIGN

BLAU PHASE I, 28 JUNE–15 JULY 1942

Generalfeldmarschall von Bock had hoped to begin *Blau* on 26 or 27 June, but heavy rains forced a temporary postponement. As it was, many units earmarked for the offensive were either still in transit or not ready to commence operations. Indeed, only eight of Heeresgruppe Süd's 68 divisions would participate on the first day of the grand offensive. Alerted by the Reichel incident, General-leytenant Filipp I. Golikov did his best to conduct spoiling attacks to disrupt German preparations. On the evening of 26 June, a surprise artillery strike by 13th Army inflicted 68 casualties upon 95.Infanterie-Division, including a battalion commander. The next day, the 2nd Air Army conducted multiple bomber attacks on German troop concentrations.

German infantry advance into a Russian village in the opening days of *Blau*. Initially, the Soviet Bryansk and South-Western fronts put up stiff resistance and yielded ground only slowly. However, this changed once 4.Panzer-Armee broke through the seam between the two Soviet fronts. (Süddeutsche Zeitung, 00384581)

On the night of 27/28 June, IV.Fliegerkorps bombed targets behind Golikov's front lines, hoping to disrupt enemy communications just prior to the kick-off. At 0315hrs on 28 June, Generaloberst Hermann Hoth's 4.Panzer-Armee opened *Blau* with a 30-minute artillery bombardment against Soviet front-line positions just east of the Tim River. The Germans chose this 60km-wide sector since it was the boundary between General-major Nikolai P. Pukhov's 13th Army and General-major Mikhail A. Parsegov's 40th Army. During the artillery preparation, German infantry from 4.Panzer-Armee and 2.Armee's LV.Armee-Korps began crossing the shallow, 25m-wide Tim River, and then proceeded to clear Soviet trenches on the opposite bank. Both Soviet armies had deployed their infantry in some depth, and their defences were not easily breached. Intense Soviet artillery fire pounded the crossing sites. However, once the sun came up, VIII.Fliegerkorps' Stukas began pulverizing the Soviet defences with pinpoint dive-bombing attacks. Within hours, German *Pioniere* were able to begin building pontoon bridges over the Tim in several places, which enabled armoured cars and support weapons to cross. In General Wilibald von Langermann und Erlenkamp's sector, 9.Panzer-Division also succeeded in capturing an intact railway bridge across the Tim. By 1000hrs, Hoth

Operation *Blau*, Phase I

1. 28 June 1942: Hoth's 4.Panzer-Armee begins *Blau* with the XXIV.Panzer-Korps and XXXXVIII.Panzer-Korps attacking the boundary between the Bryansk Front's 13th and 40th armies. The German panzer spearheads advance up to 30km on the first day.
2. The Soviet 13th Army creates a firm defence around Livny, which stops the advance of the German XIII.Armee-Korps.
3. 30 June: Stalin orders the Bryansk Front to mount an immediate counter-attack with all available armour. The Bryansk Front commits four tank corps (1st, 4th, 16th and 17th) to try to stop Hoth's panzers with a counter-attack near Kastornoye. However, the improvised Soviet armoured attack is a failure, and the Germans achieve a significant tactical victory.
4. 30 June: Paulus' 6.Armee joins the offensive, with XXXX.Panzer-Korps attacking the 21st Army, supported by two infantry corps. The 6.Armee advances, but does not achieve a complete breakthrough for two days.
5. 2 July: Tim falls to the Hungarian III Corps.
6. 3 July: The VIII.Armee-Korps advances to Novy Oskol.
7. 3 July: The XXIV.Panzer-Korps outflanks Kastornoye to the north, while XXXXVIII.Panzer-Korps envelops it from the south.
8. 3 July: The 21st and 40th armies begin retreating towards the Oskol River, but a number of divisions are cut off.
9. 4 July: VIII.Armee-Korps from 6.Armee links up with XXXXVIII.Panzer-Korps near Stary Oskol, while XXXX.Panzer-Korps begins pushing east.
10. 4 July: XXXXVIII.Panzer-Korps dashes forwards and seizes a bridge across the Don at Semiluki, then establishes a second bridgehead near Ust'ye.
11. 5 July: Despite efforts by 18th Tank Corps, the Germans capture most of Voronezh.
12. 5 July: XXIV.Panzer-Korps is forced to fend off repeated Soviet counter-attacks by the Bryansk Front against Hoth's left flank.

committed his armour: von Langermann's XXIV.Panzer-Korps on the left and General Werner Kempf's XXXXVIII.Panzer-Korps on the right. By the end of the day, the LV.Armee-Korps reported that it had captured 548 prisoners and taken 218 bunkers.

Once the Germans had a substantial force of tanks across the Tim, three of the Soviet front-line rifle divisions (15th, 121st and 160th) in their path were either crushed or shoved aside. Only the 212th Rifle Division, dug in around the town of Tim, was able to make a stand. The Hungarian III Corps was assigned to pin this Soviet force, but otherwise the Germans decided to bypass rather than assault this strongpoint. Parsegov, commander of the 40th Army, committed his two tank brigades (14th and 170th) to support the crumbling front-line infantry units, but they could not stop the enemy advance. Likewise, Pukhov's 13th Army committed its 129th Tank Brigade in an effort to delay 95.Infanterie-Division, but seven KV heavy tanks were quickly knocked out by German assault guns. Polkovnik Sergei I. Semennikov's 14th Tank Brigade managed to conduct a fighting withdrawal to the Kshen River, but within a few days, Semennikov had been killed by a Luftwaffe air strike and his brigade dispersed. Both the 2nd Air Army and 8th Air Army responded to the German offensive with hundreds of fighter and bomber sorties, harassing the advancing German columns with Il-2 Sturmovik and Pe-2 attacks. Luftflotte 4 managed to destroy 23 enemy aircraft, but lost 15 of its own. By evening of the first day, Kempf's Panzers had pushed up to 30km into the depth of the Soviet defence, Parsegov's 40th Army was crumbling and the Bryansk Front's entire left flank had been dislocated.

Golikov, the Bryansk Front commander, immediately appealed to Stavka for assistance. Stalin ordered him to hold his ground and launch counter-attacks with the front's five reserve tank corps; from the Kremlin, it appeared that Golikov had a clear numerical superiority in armour, so withdrawal seemed out of the question. During the night of 28/29 June, Golikov ordered three of his dispersed tank corps (1st, 16th and 17th) to converge upon the town of Kastornoye on the Olym River, directly in the path of

Operation *Blau*, Phase I

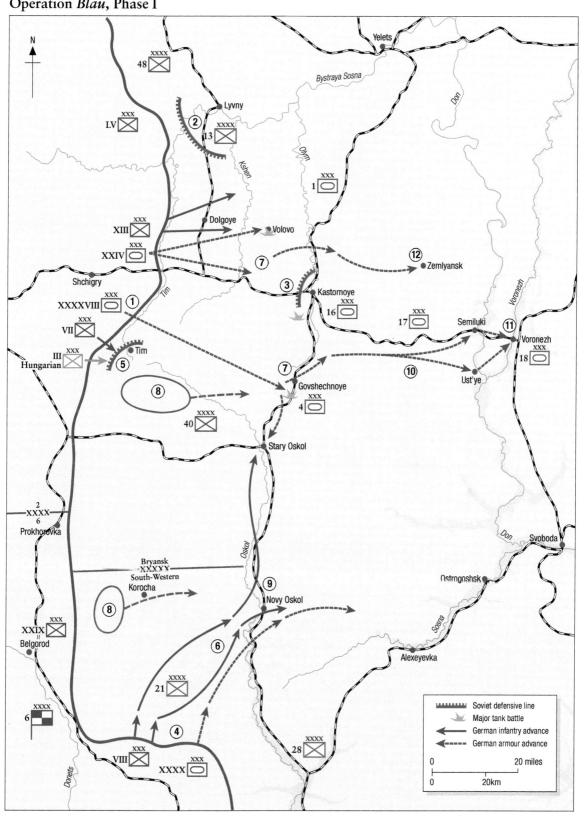

Yelets

Bystraya Sosna

Don

48 XXXX

LV XXX

Lyvny

② 13 XXXX

Kshen

Olym

1 XXX

Dolgoye

XIII XXX

Volovo

⑫ Zemlyansk

XXIV XXX

⑦

Shchigry

③

Kastornoye

16 XXX

17 XXX

Semiluki

⑪

Voronezh

18 XXX

XXXXVIII XXX ①

Tim

VII XXX

III XXX
Hungarian

Tim

⑤

⑦

⑩

Ust'ye

⑧

Govshechnoye

4 XXX

40 XXXX

Stary Oskol

2
XXXX
6
Prokhorovka

Oskol

Don

Svoboda

Bryansk
XXXXX
South-Western
Korocha

⑧

⑨

Novy Oskol

Ostrogoshsk

XXIX XXX
Belgorod

Sosna

⑥

21 XXXX

④

Alexeyevka

6 XXXX

28 XXXX

VIII XXX

XXXX

Donets

| Soviet defensive line |
| Major tank battle |
| German infantry advance |
| German armour advance |

0   20 miles

0   20km

Hoth's panzers manage to encircle some Soviet units, but the hauls of prisoners were much smaller than in 1941. Nevertheless, three Soviet armies were decimated in the initial stages of *Blau*, and the South-Western Front was forced to retreat to avoid annihilation. (Author's collection)

Italian soldiers examine a pair of knocked-out American-made M3 medium tanks in July 1942. The South-Western Front was equipped with a number of American and British-made tanks, which usually served in independent tank brigades supporting the field armies. These units were often committed piecemeal into combat to try to stop enemy breakthroughs, often with poor results. (Nik Cornish@ www.stavka.org)

Hoth's oncoming Panzers, while the other two tank corps (4th and 24th) concentrated near Stary Oskol. General-major Mikhail E. Katukov's 1st Tank Corps, probably the best of the new armoured formations, approached Kastornoye from the north, while the 16th and 17th Tank corps came from the east. Altogether, over 700 Soviet and 600 German tanks were converging on Kastornoye – setting the stage for the campaign's first great tank battle. General-leytenant Yakov N. Fedorenko, commander of all the Red Army's tank forces, arrived in Voronezh as Stavka representative to coordinate the armoured counter-stroke.

Just as Hoth's Panzers were pushing eastwards from the Tim, it began to rain heavily, and the downpour continued for the next two days, hindering German air support and tactical mobility. Nevertheless, the spearheads of each *Panzer-Korps* advanced much more quickly than Golikov expected. Both sides' armoured forces blundered towards each other in the rain, without benefit of aerial reconnaissance. It was a classic meeting engagement. On 30 June, General-major Mikhail I. Pavelkin's 16th Tank Corps advanced past the village of Volokovo, 10 miles north-west of Kastornoye, and was ambushed by General Hermann Balck's 11.Panzer-Division. The German tanks, backed up by 8.8cm Flak guns, proceeded to shoot up Pavelkin's tanks at 1,000m; in two days of skirmishing, 16th Tank Corps lost 40 of its 181 tanks. Katukov's 1st Tank Corps tried to intervene from the north with a single tank brigade, but was also repulsed with significant losses. Golikov rushed the 284th Rifle Division and other elements to Kastornoye, which temporarily halted the German advance. Given the lack of air support due to rainy, overcast weather, Hoth decided to pause while his infantry support caught up, before attempting to cross the Olym River. Further south, the 24.Panzer-Division and Infanterie-Division Grossdeutschland bypassed the knot

of Soviet resistance in Tim and sliced deep into the enemy's depth, reaching the village of Gorshechnoye, 35km south of Kastornoye.

Neither Golikov nor Fedorenko were able to coordinate the mass of Soviet armour converging upon Kastornoye. Instead, each corps attacked as individual brigade-size groups, often without air or artillery support. Pavelkin's 16th Tank Corps was typical: the formation had only been in existence for four weeks, its constituent brigades had never worked together and the corps staff was inexperienced. General-major Nikolai V. Feklenko's 17th Tank Corps misplaced its combat support units and simply ran out of fuel before reaching the front. Caught immobilized in the open by Kempf's XXXXVIII.Panzer-Korps, Feklenko's corps lost (or abandoned) 141 tanks and the survivors were routed. Feklenko was immediately relieved of command. The ability of Hoth's *Panzer-Divisionen* to act in concert while the numerically superior Soviet armour opposing them fought uncoordinated, piecemeal actions led to these kinds of lopsided tactical victories. General-major Vasily A. Mishulin's 4th Tank Corps clashed with the 24.Panzer-Division near Gorshechnoye and was defeated, instead of waiting until General-major Vasily M. Badanov's 24th Tank Corps joined the attack.

On the morning of 30 June, General Paulus' 6.Armee joined the offensive by committing General Georg Stumme's XXXX.Panzer-Korps and the VIII. Armee-Korps against General-major Aleksei I. Danilov's 21st Army. Stumme's panzers attacked with air support, but without the benefit of surprise, and ran into unusually tough resistance. The 23.Panzer-Division was slowed by mines and fierce anti-tank fire, losing ten tanks and a regimental commander on the first day of the offensive. The 3.Panzer-Division also had difficulty penetrating the sector held by the 15th Guards Rifle Division. By the end of the first day, 6.Armee had dented 21st Army's front, but not achieved a breakthrough, which indicated that the Red Army was learning how to channel

A mixed group of Soviet tanks (KV-1 on left, T-34 on right), with limited infantry support, prepare to counter-attack Hoth's panzers. Despite a large numerical superiority, the Soviet armoured formations failed to achieve any success in the large-scale tank battles west of Voronezh in early July 1942. (Nik Cornish@www.stavka.org)

German troops from 305.Infanterie-Division advance cautiously into the train station at Chernyanka on 2 July 1942. The Soviet 21st Army was already in full retreat to avoid encirclement, and resistance in front of 6.Armee began to dissipate. (Süddeutsche Zeitung, 00384527)

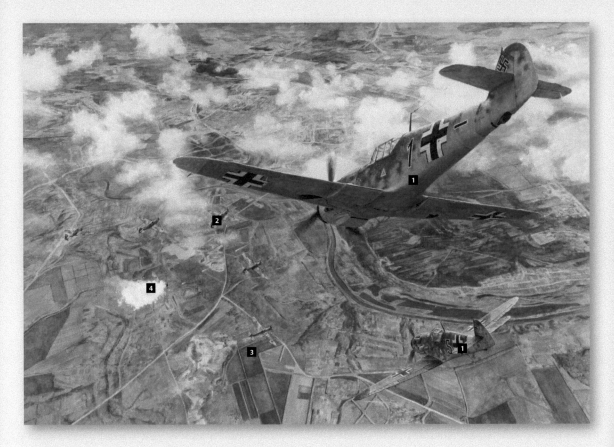

SLAUGHTER OF THE 1ST FIGHTER AVIATION ARMY, 5 JULY 1942 (PP. 40–41)

On 1 July 1942, the GKO decided to form two new aviation armies, in order to provide a fighter reserve that could be committed to critical sectors to gain air superiority. Within days, General-mayor Yevgeniy M. Beletskiy was given command of the 1st Fighter Aviation Army, which was immediately dispatched to the Yelets sector to support the counter-attack led by the 5th Tank Army. The Luftwaffe was already grinding down the Bryansk Front's 2nd Air Army in desperate combat, and Stavka thought that additional numbers from 1st Fighter Aviation Army could tip the air balance in the Soviet favour. However, the units assigned to 1st Fighter Aviation Army had not operated together before, and some units were coming from as far as Archangel. Five of the regiments assigned to 1st Fighter Aviation Army were equipped with the British-built Hurricane fighter, and two regiments were equipped with the MiG-3. When Beletskiy's 1st Fighter Aviation Army began assembling in the Yelets area on 4 July, it had 231 operational aircraft.

The 1st Fighter Aviation Army was immediately committed to combat on the morning of 5 July, and quickly ran into the Luftwaffe's

veteran pilots from Jagdgeschwader 3 between Voronezh and Terbuny. The Hurricane IIC fighter was slower than the German Bf 109F-2 and F-4 models, and also had an inferior rate of climb, which put it at a disadvantage. However, it was the German edge in pilot training that proved decisive: on the first day, 1st Fighter Aviation Army lost dozens of fighters in a series of lopsided aerial battles.

In this scene, a pair of German Bf-109Fs (1) conduct a slashing attack into a group of Soviet Hurricanes (2). One Hurricane peels off with its wing shattered by cannon fire (3), while a second bursts into flames (4). In contrast, the Luftwaffe lost only two fighters in aerial combat on this day. Fire and smoke are visible on the ground, from fighting near the city.

Heavy aerial combat continued over the next several days, but by 12 July, 1st Fighter Aviation Army had been reduced to only 66 operational fighters. Two weeks later, 1st Fighter Aviation Army was disbanded, and its remaining fighters distributed to other units. The inability of the VVS to gain air superiority over the critical Voronezh sector contributed to the failure of the Bryansk Front's counter-offensive.

and delay enemy armour. Stumme attacked again on 1 July, making small gains, but still unable to gain a real breakthrough. Instead, it was the infantry of General Walter Heitz's VIII.Armee-Korps that broke through the 21st Army front on 1 July, with the 305. and 376. Infanterie divisions in the lead. Timoshenko immediately committed his armoured reserve – General-major Petr E. Shurov's 13th Tank Corps – against Heitz's infantry. Amazingly, the German infantry divisions repulsed the Soviet tanks with their organic Panzerjäger. The next day, Heitz's infantry reached Novy Oskol, and threatened to isolate the Soviet troops still holding out in Tim and parts of the 21st Army. Although General-leytenant Dmitri I. Riabyshev's 28th Army was holding firm on the right flank of 6.Armee's penetration, it was also at risk of being enveloped by Stumme's panzers.

Aerial combat resumed on 30 June as the rain began to subside. Initially, Luftflotte 4 was surprised by the aggressiveness of 2nd Air Army and 8th Air Army, which committed large numbers of aircraft into the fight. On this day, Luftflotte 4 lost 23 aircraft, against about 30-plus for the Soviets. Yet only a few Soviet fighter units – the ones with a cadre of experienced pilots – were inflicting most of the casualties on the Luftwaffe, while the other regiments achieved little.

Panzers from 3.Infanterie-Division (mot.) cross the Don River at Semiluki on 7 July 1942. The Germans were able to 'bounce' the river before the Soviets could establish a proper defence, then pushed rapidly into the heart of the lightly defended city. (Bundesarchiv, Bild 101I-216-0435-37. Foto: Koch)

Soviet bomber regiments, with Boston and Pe-2 bombers, were flung with reckless abandon against the German spearheads, suffering heavy casualties. Meanwhile, hundreds of Il-2 Sturmoviks were kept in reserve near Moscow, just in case the Germans made a move towards the capital. After a few days of intense aerial combat in early July, the *Experten* of Luftflotte 4 began to gain the upper hand. Once the skies were cleared of enemy fighters, VIII. Fliegerkorps moved in to smash enemy armoured formations.

As the weather improved on 2 July, Hoth resumed his offensive. Balck's 11.Panzer-Division crossed the Olym River 15km north of Kastornoye, while 9.Panzer-Division crossed just south of the town. Simultaneously, 24.Panzer-Division and Infanterie-Division Grossdeutschland crossed the river near Gorshechnoye and overran the headquarters of the 40th Army. Pavelkin's 16th Tank Corps attempted to block Balck's Panzers, but was badly mauled and retreated in disorder. Likewise, Mishulin's 4th Tank Corps was unable to stop Kempf's XXXXVIII.Panzer-Korps. Having crossed the Olym, the two German armoured spearheads now began to close around the Soviet forces grouped around Kastornoye. The only place where the German advance was halted was on the left flank of the penetration, where Pukhov's 13th Army successfully blocked the LV.Armee-Korps from reaching its objective of Lyvny. Reluctantly, on 3 July, Stavka authorized the 21st, 28th and 40th armies to withdraw in order to avoid encirclement. The strongpoint in Tim fell to the Hungarian III Corps, and the Soviets began a fighting retreat from the Olym back towards Voronezh. Once it was clear that Soviet forces were in retreat, Hoth shifted to pursuit, while 6.Armee pushed north in an effort to cut off withdrawing Soviet units. On 4 July, the 387.Infanterie-Division, which was temporarily attached to the Hungarian Second Army, fought its way into Stary Oskol and soon linked up with Heitz's VIII.Armee-Korps. Elements of

A T-34 tank destroyed near Voronezh, July 1942. The tank battles in this region and in the Don Bend were some of the largest and most intense of World War II, but they generally get little mention in most histories due to the catastrophic defeat of three Soviet tank armies. Stalin forced his generals to throw their armour into meat-grinder battles with little coordination or preparation, resulting in one fiasco after another. (Bundesarchiv, Bild 169-0453)

at least five Soviet rifle divisions were caught within the pincers, but most of the personnel escaped, albeit without their equipment. Golikov deployed General-major Ivan P. Korchagin's 17th Tank Corps to assist the rearguard and shield Voronezh, but the Soviet retreat to the Don turned into a disorderly mess. Despite the fact that his units were badly outnumbered and well in front of their supporting infantry, Hoth gambled and sent Kempf's panzers towards Voronezh, while XXIV.Panzer-Korps harried the Soviet retreat.

The retreat of the Soviet 21st, 28th and 40th armies turned into a shambles because Soviet command and control was breaking down and the Germans were moving too swiftly. Riabyshev's 28th Army was the most fortunate, since it managed to save about 50 per cent of its personnel, but the army was too decimated to make a stand on the Oskol River. By 3 July, the advance elements of 6.Armee were already across the river and had captured Novy Oskol. Danilov's 21st Army had to try and fight its way out through Paulus' 6.Armee, which proved difficult. Danilov used Shurov's 13th Tank Corps as a battering ram, but the formation was smashed and Shurov killed. Nevertheless, Danilov succeeded in breaking out with small groups of survivors. Likewise, Parsegov's 40th Army managed to exfiltrate about half its personnel to the Don, but it had no combat-capable units left by 4 July; Stalin relieved Parsegov of command. While it is true that the German pincers failed to take any large haul of prisoners west of the Don, it is also true that two Soviet armies had been shattered and a third decimated. A very large hole had been blown in the Soviet front, and the only units available to plug the gap proved ineffective due to the breakdown of command and control at the front level. Golikov transferred his headquarters to Voronezh to try to restore order, but this proved too late.

Hoth took full advantage of the Soviet confusion and disorder. Generalleutnant Walter Hörnlein's Infanterie-Division Grossdeutschland easily bypassed Korchagin's 17th Tank Corps and reached the Don River by dusk on 4 July. Oberleutnant Carl-Ludwig Blumenthal's 7.Kompanie was in the lead, and at 1930hrs, he found the road bridge over the Don near Semiluki guarded by only a handful of Soviet troops. In a daring assault, Blumenthal led his men across the bridge, routed the defenders and then removed the demolition charges; Blumenthal was awarded the Ritterkreuz des Eisernen Kreuzes for his feat. Amazingly, Golikov had very few combat troops actually in Voronezh, and Blumenthal's coup had opened the door. Making the situation even worse, 24.Panzer-Division managed to cross the Don on the morning of 5 July. Although Hoth was reluctant to fight in a major urban area, Kempf immediately sent 24.Panzer-Division into the suburbs of Voronezh, and encountered only light resistance from militia detachments and anti-aircraft units. Golikov managed to rush up some tanks from the 18th Tank Corps to stiffen the defence, but two tank brigades were caught in column march in the streets of the city and destroyed by

Panzerjäger. On the night of 5/6 June, Soviet forces evacuated Voronezh, establishing a new line in the suburbs on the eastern bank of the Voronezh River. The next day, the Germans completed the occupation of the city, thereby achieving one of the major objectives of *Blau I*.

Astonished by the inability of Golikov's forces to seriously delay Hoth's advance, Stavka immediately began sending more reinforcements from the RVGK to repair the gap between the Bryansk and South-Western fronts. Stalin decided to play his potential trump card – General-major Aleksandr I. Liziukov's 5th Tank Army – to lead a major counter-attack against Hoth's Panzers. Liziukov, a veteran commander and Hero of the Soviet Union, was provided with three tank corps (2nd, 7th and 11th) and additional forces for the counter-stroke, amounting to over 641 tanks. Stavka ordered Liziukov to conduct a slashing attack into the left flank of Hoth's 4.Panzer-Armee and advance nearly 60km to sever its lines of communications. In addition, the VVS committed over 200 of its fighter reserves from the Moscow region to create a new formation known as the 1st Fighter Aviation Army, which was intended to gain air superiority over the Voronezh sector. While impressive on paper, Stalin forced Liziukov into premature action, with virtually no planning conducted prior to battle. Despite the fact that only two tank brigades of General-major Pavel. A. Rotmistrov's 7th Tank Corps reached the assembly areas in time, Liziukov duly began his counter-offensive at dawn on 6 July. Rotmistrov was one of the Red Army's veteran tank commanders, and his two brigades succeeded in pushing back a *Kampfgruppe* from 9.Panzer-Division on the first day. On 7 July, Rotmistrov continued attacking southwards, joined by a single brigade from General-major Aleksei F. Popov's 11th Tank Corps. Recognizing the Soviet armoured threat, XXIV.Panzer-Korps shifted both its *Panzer-Divisionen* to block Liziukov, while creating a solid front with XIII. Armee-Korps on its left. However, XXIV.Panzer-Korps had no friendly units on its immediate right flank, which lay open to envelopment. Nevertheless, the German armoured units conducted a mobile delay, which slowed the Soviet advance to a crawl, while VIII.Fliegerkorps pounded Soviet tank concentrations with repeated Stuka attacks. Liziukov did not get all his forces into the fight

The rapid German advance overran some Soviet installations before they could be evacuated. Here, a train loaded with newly arrived British-built Valentine Mark III tanks has been captured before the vehicles could be offloaded. (Nik Cornish@www.stavka.org)

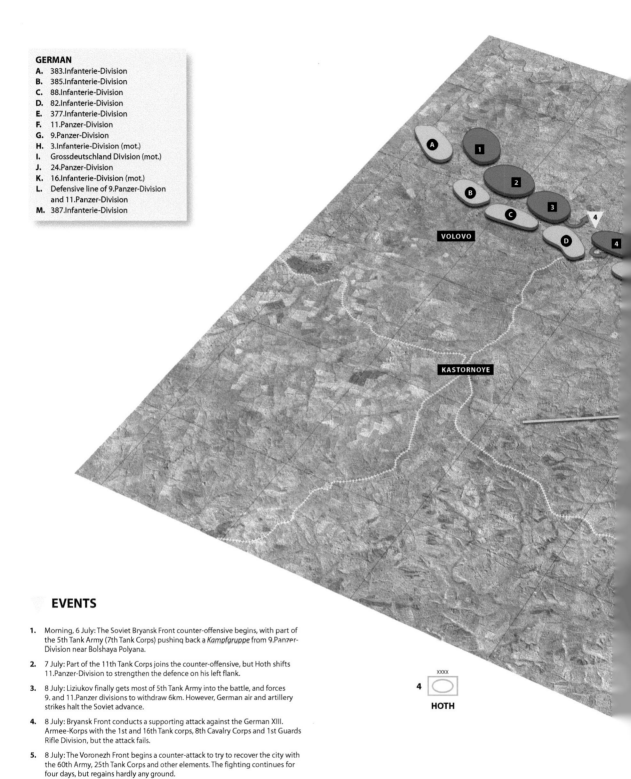

GERMAN

A. 383.Infanterie-Division
B. 385.Infanterie-Division
C. 88.Infanterie-Division
D. 82.Infanterie-Division
E. 377.Infanterie-Division
F. 11.Panzer-Division
G. 9.Panzer-Division
H. 3.Infanterie-Division (mot.)
I. Grossdeutschland Division (mot.)
J. 24.Panzer-Division
K. 16.Infanterie-Division (mot.)
L. Defensive line of 9.Panzer-Division
   and 11.Panzer-Division
M. 387.Infanterie-Division

VOLOVO

KASTORNOYE

EVENTS

1. Morning, 6 July: The Soviet Bryansk Front counter-offensive begins, with part of the 5th Tank Army (7th Tank Corps) pushing back a *Kampfgruppe* from 9.Panzer-Division near Bolshaya Polyana.

2. 7 July: Part of the 11th Tank Corps joins the counter-offensive, but Hoth shifts 11.Panzer-Division to strengthen the defence on his left flank.

3. 8 July: Liziukov finally gets most of 5th Tank Army into the battle, and forces 9. and 11.Panzer divisions to withdraw 6km. However, German air and artillery strikes halt the Soviet advance.

4. 8 July: Bryansk Front conducts a supporting attack against the German XIII. Armee-Korps with the 1st and 16th Tank corps, 8th Cavalry Corps and 1st Guards Rifle Division, but the attack fails.

5. 8 July: The Voronezh Front begins a counter-attack to try to recover the city with the 60th Army, 25th Tank Corps and other elements. The fighting continues for four days, but regains hardly any ground.

6. 9 July: The 5th Tank Army launches a major attack to break the new German line, but the 7th and 11th Tank corps suffer heavy losses, and are repulsed. Soviet attacks continue in this sector for the next two days, but achieve nothing.

7. 10 July: Hoth shifts the 387.Infanterie-Division to cover the open flank north of Zemlyansk, while the mechanized divisions in Voronezh are gradually relieved by XXIX.Armee-Korps.

8. 12 July: The 9. and 11.Panzer divisions counter-attack, driving back the 2nd and 7th Tank corps.

XXXX

4 ⬭

HOTH

Note: gridlines are shown at intervals of 20km (12.43 miles)

THE SOVIET COUNTER-OFFENSIVE AT VORONEZH, 6–12 JULY 1942

Stavka ordered the Bryansk Front to launch an immediate counter-offensive to recover the city and push in Hoth's left flank. Although stressed, the improvised German defences held, and inflicted great losses on the Soviet reserves, including the 5th Tank Army.

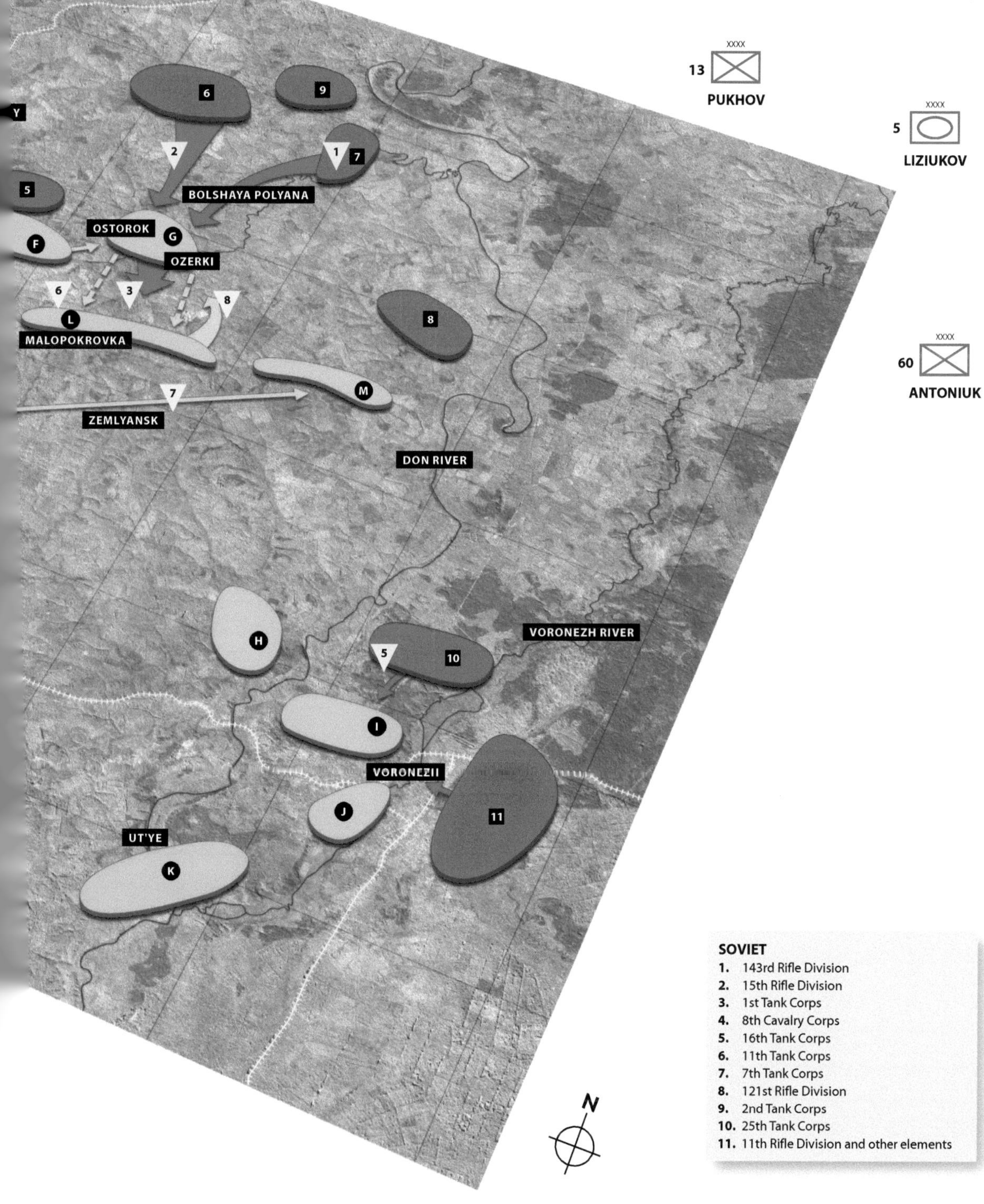

XXXX
13
PUKHOV
XXXX
5
LIZIUKOV
XXXX
60
ANTONIUK
BOLSHAYA POLYANA
OSTOROK
OZERKI
MALOPOKROVKA
ZEMLYANSK
DON RIVER
VORONEZH RIVER
VORONEZH
UT'YE
N
SOVIET
1. 143rd Rifle Division
2. 15th Rifle Division
3. 1st Tank Corps
4. 8th Cavalry Corps
5. 16th Tank Corps
6. 11th Tank Corps
7. 7th Tank Corps
8. 121st Rifle Division
9. 2nd Tank Corps
10. 25th Tank Corps
11. 11th Rifle Division and other elements

A German soldier poses in Voronezh, 1942. The Germans managed to occupy most of the city until 24 January 1943, but the garrison remained under near-continuous attack for seven months, and the Germans derived no benefit from its occupation. By the time that the Red Army recovered the city, it had been largely demolished. (Nik Cornish@ www.stavka.org)

until 8 July, by which point his losses were mounting. Nor did it help that marshy terrain in the sector chosen for the attack forced Liziukov to conduct frontal assaults. For several days, Liziukov continued to pound on the German front to no avail. The Bryansk Front tried to help with a supporting attack by Katukov's 1st Tank Corps and other units against XIII.Armee-Korps, but this effort also failed ignominiously. Furthermore, the commitment of 1st Fighter Aviation Army proved to be a disaster, with 48 of the novice pilots lost on the first day, for only two German Bf 109Fs. Consequently, it was quickly apparent that the Bryansk Front was unable to make any serious penetration into Hoth's flank.

Nevertheless, Kempf was forced to keep the bulk of his XXXXVIII.Panzer-Korps in the immediate vicinity of Voronezh in order to fend off a series of counter-attacks mounted by Golikov, using the fresh 25th Tank Corps and General-leytenant Maksim A. Antoniuk's 60th Army. Although Golikov's efforts failed, they did succeed in tying down Kempf's forces until 12 July. Hitler was perturbed that Hoth's armour was tied up for so long around Voronezh, and began to increasingly criticize von Bock's handling of his forces. Amazingly, the OKH did not recognize that Hoth was being attacked by a Soviet tank army and multiple tank corps, and instead regarded the situation as more akin to a leisurely mop-up operation. Indeed, Hitler was so insistent in adhering to the schedule and pushing on towards the south-east that he failed to appreciate that Hoth was achieving an amazing victory around Voronezh.

The protracted fighting around Voronezh led to the senior leadership on both sides making changes. On 7 July, Stavka decided to split the Bryansk Front, with the left wing becoming the new Voronezh Front under Golikov. General-mayor Nikandr E. Chibisov assumed command over the restructured Bryansk Front, and was ordered to assist Liziukov with a front-level counter-offensive against Hoth's left flank using Katukov's 1st Tank Corps and other available units. On the German side, Hitler continued to insist that Hoth's Panzers push south-east forthwith to form an outer pincer to link up with 1.Panzer-Armee in accordance with *Blau 2*. For his part, von Bock was increasingly upset by the mediocre performance of Paulus' 6.Armee, which appeared capable of making only slow advances against weak enemy resistance. In particular, von Bock noted in his diary that Paulus had difficulty establishing priorities and did not get the best results from his troops. Stumme's leadership of XXXX.Panzer-Korps was also sub-par, particularly when compared with Kempf and von Langermann. On 9 July, the OKH officially redesignated the northern wing of Heeresgruppe Süd as Heeresgruppe B. Von Bock protested this move as premature, which only increased Hitler's annoyance with him. Two days later, Führer Directive No. 43 assigned Hoth's 4.Panzer-Armee to Heeresgruppe A, reducing von Bock's command to 2.Armee, 6.Armee and the Hungarian Second Army.

Not only did Hoth fend off the Bryansk Front's counter-offensive, but he even managed to conduct a relief in place, bringing in 57.Infanterie-Division to hold Voronezh while pulling out XXIV.Panzer-Korps. The VII.Armee-Korps and Hungarian III Corps were also brought forwards to hold the flanks on either side of Voronezh. Once it became clear that Liziukov's counter-offensive was faltering, XXIV.Panzer-Korps prepared a riposte. On 12 July, von Langermann attacked with the 9. and 11.Panzer divisions, supported by numerous Stuka sorties. In two days of heavy fighting, Liziukov's 5th Tank Army was broken and thrown back in disorder. Altogether, the 5th Tank Army lost about 300 tanks, and was no longer combat effective. German armour losses totalled about 50–60 tanks in XXIV.Panzer-Korps. Enraged by the failure, Stalin ordered the 5th Tank Army disbanded and Liziukov demoted. Chibisov's attempts to support Liziukov by attacking the LV.Armee-Korps were easily repulsed; Stalin replaced Chibisov as commander of the Bryansk Front with General-leytenant Konstantin K. Rokossovsky. Golikov's efforts to recapture Voronezh also failed, so Stalin replaced Golikov with General-leytenant Nikolai F. Vatutin from the General Staff. While Rokossovsky and Vatutin were both skilled commanders, Stalin's spontaneous purge of unsuccessful front-line commanders only served to undermine Soviet tactical command and control.

In just over two weeks, von Bock's forces had advanced over 160km, shattered several Soviet armies, routed Stavka's best armoured reserves and captured a major Soviet urban centre. The Soviet Bryansk, Voronezh and South-Western fronts had suffered over 300,000 casualties, whereas Heeresgruppe A suffered only 24,000 casualties, a 12:1 exchange ratio. It was a significant operational achievement, and Hitler told Halder that, 'the Russian is finished'. Yet at this point, Hitler decided that he did not need independent-minded commanders meddling with his unfolding plans, so he relieved von Bock of command on 15 July. He then placed Generaloberst Maximilian von Weichs in command of Heeresgruppe B, while General Hans von Salmuth took over 2.Armee.

A PzKpfw III Ausf. L tank in front of the burnt-out Hotel Voronezh, Lenin Square, central Voronezh. By 7 July, the centre of this city, which had a prewar population of 326,000, had been occupied by the XXXXVIII.Panzer-Korps. (Nik Cornish@www.stavka.org)

CLEARING THE DONBASS, 16–31 JULY 1942

On 9 July, Generalfeldmarschall Wilhelm List's Heeresgruppe A had joined the summer offensive by attacking the remainder of Marshal Semyon K. Timoshenko's South-Western Front with Generaloberst Ewald von Kleist's 1.Panzer-Armee. Two days later, 17.Armee attacked the Southern Front. The entire Soviet front line between the Sea of Azov and Voronezh was now under assault. Stavka had already authorized Timoshenko to withdraw all four of his armies to prevent their destruction, which dashed Hitler's hopes of encircling large Soviet forces between the Don and the Donets. Attempted envelopments at Boguchar, then Millerovo, yielded only about 14,000 prisoners. Although badly battered, Timoshenko's forces slipped away to fight another day. On the night of 9/10 July, Stavka decided to commit three reserve armies (1st, 5th and 7th, which would become the 64th, 63rd and 62nd armies) to reinforce Timoshenko, although it would take about ten days to deploy them to the front. On 12 July, Timoshenko's South-Western Front was redesignated as the Stalingrad Front, and since the three new reserve armies were already en route, Timoshenko was ordered to transfer the 9th, 28th and 38th armies to the Southern Front. Once the reserve armies reached the front, Stavka directed Timoshenko to establish a firm defence in the Donbass region with General-major Vladimir Ia. Kolpakchi's 62nd Army, forward of the Don, in order to block the approaches to Stalingrad.

Heeresgruppe B reorganized itself as it began advancing towards the Donbass. Von Salmuth's 2.Armee was deployed to defend the left flank of the army group from Voronezh to the vicinity of Lyvny. Since this sector faced constant Soviet counter-attacks, both the 9. and 11.Panzer divisions remained to support von Salmuth. Von Langermann's XXIV.Panzer-Korps moved east to support 6.Armee, but only with the 3. and 16.Infanterie divisions (mot.) – leaving Paulus without significant armour support. The Hungarian III Corps took over a sector of the Don south of Voronezh, but the rest of the Hungarian Second Army had not yet reached the front. Hoth's 4.Panzer-Armee (XXXX. and XXXXVIII.Panzer-Korps) was also directed into the Donbass, but to support Heeresgruppe A's operations, not Paulus'

German bicycle-mounted infantry pause during the advance into the Donbass in mid-July 1942. Heavy rains hindered the German advance, and the troops are wearing their camouflaged Zeltbahn ponchos to ward off the rain. Even in some motorized units, fuel shortages made it difficult to move infantry forwards, and bicycles were better than nothing – but clearly the muddy track is not conducive to bicycle movement. (Süddeutsche Zeitung, 00384578)

Advance into the Donbass

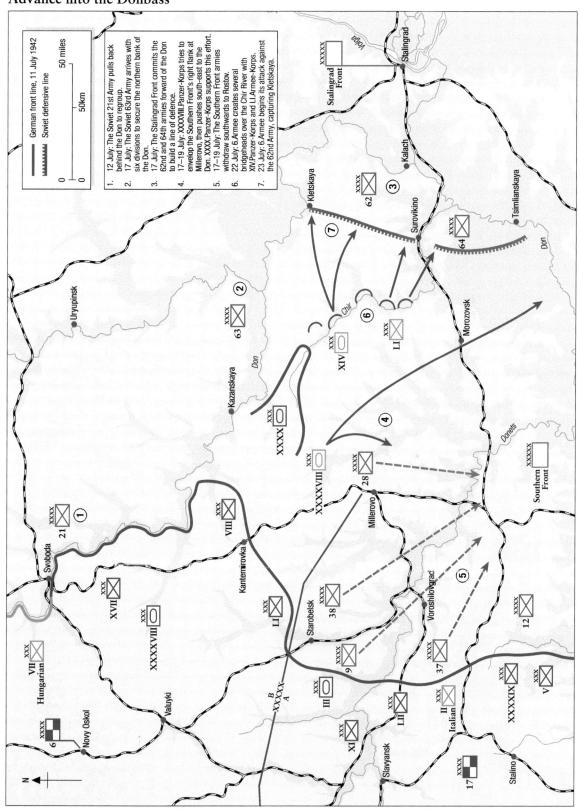

German front line, 11 July 1942

Soviet defensive line

0   50km

0   50 miles

1. 12 July: The Soviet 21st Army pulls back behind the Don to regroup.
2. 17 July: The Soviet 63rd Army arrives with six divisions to secure the northern bank of the Don.
3. 17 July: The Stalingrad Front commits the 62nd and 64th armies forward of the Don to build a line of defence.
4. 17–19 July: XXXVIII.Panzer-Korps tries to envelop the Southern Front's right flank at Millerovo, then pushes south-east to the Don. XXX.Panzer-Korps supports this effort.
5. 17–19 July: The Southern Front armies withdraw southwards to Rostov.
6. 22 July: 6.Armee creates several bridgeheads over the Chir River with XIV.Panzer-Korps and LI.Armee-Korps.
7. 23 July: 6.Armee begins its attack against the 62nd Army, capturing Kletskaya.

6.Armee. Consequently, the main German focus in mid-July shifted from the Voronezh sector to the Rostov sector, and the advance towards Stalingrad was a lesser priority.

Timoshenko's South-Western Front headquarters was nearly overrun in Rossosh on 7 July, but otherwise the retreating Soviet formations were able to stay ahead of their pursuers. Danilov's battered 21st Army, reduced to only a single rifle division, slipped across the Don south-east of Svoboda, thereby gaining a respite. General-leytenant Vasily I. Kuznetsov's fresh 63rd Army and the 3rd Guards Cavalry Corps began arriving on the northern bank of the Don, to establish a solid defensive front all along the river. With Hoth's 4.Panzer-Armee swinging south to envelop Riabyshev's 28th Army near Millerovo, Paulus' 6.Armee was reduced to just two divisions (113.Infanterie-Division and 100.Jäger-Division) from Heitz's VIII.Armee-Korps marching slowly towards the Chir River. As Paulus advanced along the west bank of the Don, he was obliged to peel off four infantry divisions (62., 79., 336. and 384.) to guard his left flank. Furthermore, Paulus' advance was plagued by fuel shortages and the difficulty of finding water in this arid steppe region. Temperatures soared to over 100° F (37.8° C), and the horses pulling Paulus' artillery could not go very far or very fast without adequate water. Furthermore, 6.Armee was essentially moving cross-country and not following any railways or major roads, which inflicted great wear and tear on the wheeled logistic vehicles. Consequently, it took the vanguard of 6.Armee ten days to advance 100km against negligible opposition. It was not until the evening of 21 July that Paulus was able to get a sizeable force to the Chir River, consisting of Heitz's VIII.Armee-Korps and General Walter Seydlitz-Kurzbach's LI.Armee-Korps (44., 71. and 297.Infanterie divisions). Concerned by Paulus' lethargic advance, on 20 July, the OKH transferred General Gustav von Wietersheim's XIV.Panzer-Korps from 1.Panzer-Armee to support Paulus' crossing of the Chir. By the morning of 22 July, 6.Armee had created several bridgeheads across the Chir.

German troops prepare to cross a water obstacle with a small inflatable raft. The Germans had learned a great deal about tactical water crossing since the 1939 Polish campaign, and by mid-1942, they had developed well-oiled drills for this most difficult tactical operation. Again and again, the Soviets failed to properly use river lines to bolster their defence. (Süddeutsche Zeitung, 00384601)

A column of German armour (probably from 16.Panzer-Division) advances between the Don and Donets, July 1942. Note the dust raised by the movement across the dry, waterless steppe. The PzKpfw III Ausf. L, with its long 5cm gun, was a significant improvement over the models used in *Barbarossa*. (Süddeutsche Zeitung, 00384663)

Paulus' slow advance enabled Kolpakchi's 62nd Army to build a thin defensive line in the great bend of the Don, about 50km west of Stalingrad. He deployed four rifle divisions on a 90km-wide front between Kletskaya on the Don and Surovikino, with one rifle division deployed in second echelon. Kolpakchi had the 40th Tank Brigade and six independent tank battalions in reserve, totaling 277 tanks. In addition, Kolpakchi's left flank was supposed to be tied in with General-leytenant Vasily I. Chuikov's 64th Army south of the Chir River. However, the 62nd Army was in an exposed position in open terrain, trying to hold an overly wide sector. Furthermore, the Luftwaffe's aggressive battlefield interdiction efforts seriously interfered with the deployment of Stavka's reserve armies by damaging several rail stations around Stalingrad and sinking numerous vessels on the Volga. The Soviets took the risk of running troop trains towards Stalingrad in daylight hours, which led to heavy casualties when Stukas appeared. Although General-major Timofei T. Khriukhin's 8th Air Army had been forced to displace eastwards, his formation received priority for replacements, and his fighter units made a valiant effort to fend off the Luftwaffe air raids. Nevertheless, the Luftwaffe did succeed in delaying the deployment of Chuikov's 64th Army. Khriukhin's 8th Air Army was able to mount its own bombing and strafing attacks to slow down the approaching German 6.Armee.

On the morning of 22 July, Paulus began his advance across the Chir River, with the three divisions of von Wietersheim's XIV.Panzer-Korps in the lead. Kolpakchi had only deployed outpost units along the Chir, so the German motorized units were able to get across the river and deploy without much hindrance. The only major problem was dwindling fuel supplies, which forced each division commander to leave some units out of the fight in order to provide all fuel to the spearhead units. At 0200hrs on 23 July, von Wietersheim's XIV.Panzer-Korps attacked with 3. and 60.Infanterie divisions (mot.) in the north and 16.Panzer-Division in the south. The two German motorized divisions struck Kolpakchi's line at its weakly held north end, capturing the lynchpin of Kletskaya by 0900hrs, then fended off a

DESPERATE STAND NEAR COLLECTIVE FARM NO. 2, 1700HRS, 25 JULY 1942 (PP. 54–55)

Before dawn on 25 July, the German XIV.Panzer-Korps sent a raiding group to envelop the right flank of the Soviet 62nd Army and, perhaps, to capture the bridge over the Don at Kalach. The group comprised mixed elements from both the 3. and 60.Infanterie divisions (mot.). By late morning, Major Josef Fau's Kradschützen-Bataillon 53 managed to occupy the village of Lozhki and the Collective Farm No. 2, just 8.5km north-west of the Kalach bridge. Had the Germans not been plagued by fuel shortages, they might have pressed on to seize the bridge. Instead, Fau had to content himself with ordering his attached howitzer battery to begin shelling Soviet traffic on the bridge. General-major Efim G. Pushkin, deputy commander of the Stalingrad Front, was on the spot and he reacted immediately, ordering General-major Trofim I. Tanaschishin's 13th Tank Corps (part of 1st Tank Army) to cross the bridge and drive the German forces out of Lozhki and away from Kalach. Quickly improvising an attack with just two brigades – the 55th and 56th Tank brigades – Tanaschishin's 13th Tank Corps jumped off by mid-afternoon. Covered by a swirling dust storm, the two brigades deployed on line with a total of more than 80 tanks, then rushed the German line. Fau's Kradschützen-Bataillon 53 was not prepared to stop a massed tank assault and fell back, yielding Lozhki, Collective Farm No. 2 and the nearby Hill 169.4.

However, Fau had prepared a second line of defence, based upon a pair of 88mm Flak guns and a single platoon of PzKpfw III tanks. The 88mm guns engaged the oncoming Soviet tanks, destroying at least four, before the guns were disabled by return fire. Disaster beckoned for the Germans, as the Soviet mass of armour continued to roll on, led by the 56th Tank Brigade, destroying enemy wheeled vehicles and scattering Fau's battalion. Suddenly, the lead Soviet tank battalion began to receive accurate fire from its flank, from Stabsfeldwebel Wilhelm Wolf's tank platoon, which was deployed in reverse slope positions.

This scene shows a PzKpfw III tank from Wolf's platoon in the foreground (1), looking south-east towards the approaching 56th Tank Brigade tanks (2). Some of the Soviet tanks have already been hit, and are burning (3). Behind the Soviet armoured group, a pair of destroyed German 88mm Flak guns can be seen (4). The Don River is visible in the distance (5), along with deep balkas (ravines) behind the Soviet formation. The buildings of Collective Farm No. 2 can also be seen smouldering in the background (6).

Although all of Wolf's PzKpfw III tanks were immobilized by lack of fuel, their gunnery was superb, knocking out one Soviet tank after another. Two Soviet tank battalion commanders were killed and about 20 more tanks disabled, causing the Soviets to fall back. Although Wolf's platoon had not suffered any losses in the tank action, his platoon was virtually out of armour-piercing rounds – but the Soviets were not aware of this. By this bold manoeuvre, the German XIV.Panzer-Korps had succeeded in isolating a large portion of the Soviet 62nd Army in the Don Bend, but the Soviet armoured counter-attack was stopped only by the narrowest of margins.

counter-attack by the 40th Tank Brigade, which lost 21 tanks. Further south, Generalleutnant Hans-Valentin Hube's 16.Panzer-Division sliced through the centre of Kolpakchi's 62nd Army. The 192nd Rifle Division, assigned to protect the right flank of the 62nd Army, began retreating to the Sirotinskaya bridgehead, which opened the door to further German exploitation of Kolpakchi's now open flank. However, the German panzer units had nearly exhausted their fuel supplies, which robbed them of much of their mobility.

Just as 6.Armee's attack in the Don Bend was beginning, Stalin decided to relieve Timoshenko of command and replace him with General-leytenant Vasily N. Gordov. Stalin had lost confidence in Timoshenko since the Kharkov disaster, but the timing of his relief could not have been worse. Nor was Gordov a marked improvement: he had limited aptitude for senior command, but his main attribute was that he was backed by Georgy Malenkov, a senior member of the GKO. Stavka ordered Gordov to hold the line in the eastern Donbass and prevent any enemy penetration towards Stalingrad, but he was already faced with a serious breach of his outer defences on his first day in command of Stalingrad Front.

Meanwhile, by 23 July, Heeresgruppe A was beginning to fight its way into Rostov, and it looked to Hitler like Soviet forces in the south were on the verge of complete collapse. At the very least, the Soviets no longer had a continuous front, which encouraged Hitler and Halder to think that a decisive moment in the campaign had arrived. In his diary, Halder gloated that, 'the enemy is running for dear life'. Although *Blau* had specified that the offensive should be conducted in distinct phases, so the Germans could concentrate air and logistic support behind the main effort, Hitler now believed this requirement was no longer necessary. Consequently, he issued Führer Directive No. 45, which specified that Heeresgruppe A would advance into the Caucasus (redesignated as Operation *Edelweiss*) while, simultaneously, Heeresgruppe B would create a defensive front along the northern bend of the Don and advance to capture Stalingrad (designated Operation *Fischreiher*). German air and logistic support – already overstretched – would now be split

On 27 July, the Stalingrad Front committed the 158th Tank Brigade into the ongoing battle in the great bend of the Don, in an effort to link up with encircled elements of the 62nd Army. However, the hastily ordered attack was easily smashed by German anti-tank and Flak guns, with 28 KV-1 tanks knocked out. (Nik Cornish@www.stavka.org)

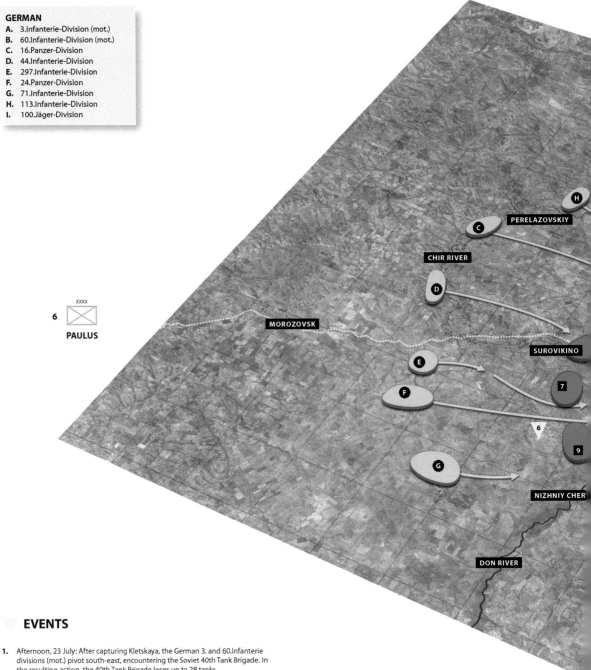

GERMAN
A. 3.Infanterie-Division (mot.)
B. 60.Infanterie-Division (mot.)
C. 16.Panzer-Division
D. 44.Infanterie-Division
E. 297.Infanterie-Division
F. 24.Panzer-Division
G. 71.Infanterie-Division
H. 113.Infanterie-Division
I. 100.Jäger-Division

6
PAULUS

PERELAZOVSKIY
CHIR RIVER
MOROZOVSK
SUROVIKINO
NIZHNIY CHER
DON RIVER

▼ EVENTS

1. Afternoon, 23 July: After capturing Kletskaya, the German 3. and 60.Infanterie divisions (mot.) pivot south-east, encountering the Soviet 40th Tank Brigade. In the resulting action, the 40th Tank Brigade loses up to 28 tanks.

2. The 192nd Rifle Division, protecting the right flank of 62nd Army, retreats to the Sirotinskaya bridgehead.

3. 24 July: The Soviet 13th Tank Corps engages 16.Panzer-Division near Manolin. However, the lead *Kampfgruppe* from 16.Panzer-Division reaches the Liska River. One-third of the 62nd Army is now isolated.

4. Morning, 25 July: Two *Kampfgruppen* from 3. and 60.Infanterie divisions (mot.) move to envelop the 62nd Army's right flank, and they bring the Kalach bridge under artillery fire. Most of the German vehicles in these *Kampfgruppen* run out of fuel.

5. Afternoon, 25 July: Stalingrad Front commits the 28th Tank Corps across the Kalach bridge to prevent the Germans from surrounding Group Zhuravlev (33rd Guards Rifle Division and part of 62nd Army). The German vanguard, dubbed Kampfgruppe Schlömer, is isolated, but repulses several tank attacks by 28th Tank Corps.

6. 26 July: The XXIV.Panzer-Korps and LI.Armee-Korps attack the right flank of 64th Army and reach the Chir, but do not achieve a link up with the XIV.Panzer-Korps vanguard.

7. 26–27 July: The 28th Tank Corps mounts two major attacks against Kampfgruppe Schlömer, inflicting some losses, but in turn losing over 70 tanks. This area becomes a tank graveyard, but the German supply situation is desperate.

8. 28 July: A *Kampfgruppe* from 16.Panzer-Division finally links up with Kampfgruppe Schlömer, and provides some resupply. However, the Germans have temporarily lost the tactical initiative.

9. 31 July: Group Zhuravlev conducts a breakout, and 5,000 personnel succeed in reaching Soviet lines.

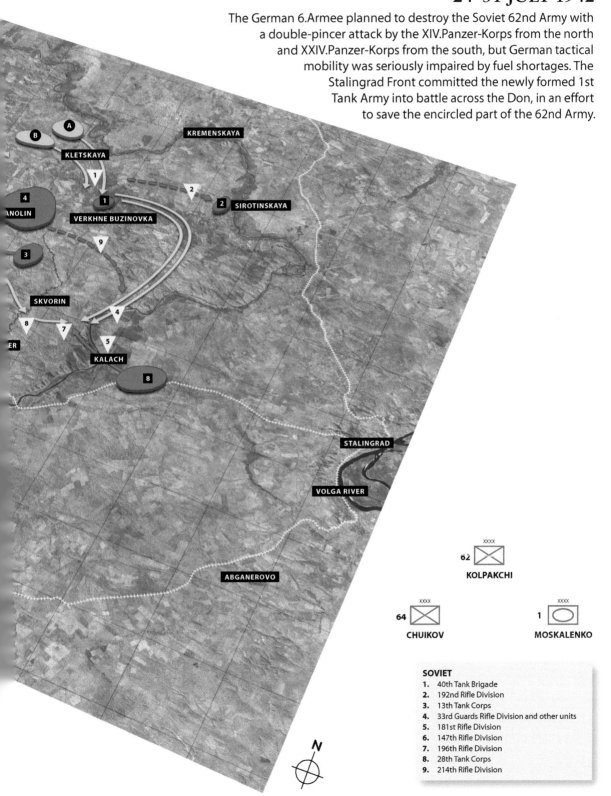

BATTLE OF THE DON BEND, 24–31 JULY 1942

The German 6.Armee planned to destroy the Soviet 62nd Army with a double-pincer attack by the XIV.Panzer-Korps from the north and XXIV.Panzer-Korps from the south, but German tactical mobility was seriously impaired by fuel shortages. The Stalingrad Front committed the newly formed 1st Tank Army into battle across the Don, in an effort to save the encircled part of the 62nd Army.

KREMENSKAYA

KLETSKAYA

VERKHNE BUZINOVKA

SIROTINSKAYA

ANOLIN

SKVORIN

KALACH

STALINGRAD

VOLGA RIVER

ABGANEROVO

62 KOLPAKCHI

64 CHUIKOV

1 MOSKALENKO

SOVIET
1. 40th Tank Brigade
2. 192nd Rifle Division
3. 13th Tank Corps
4. 33rd Guards Rifle Division and other units
5. 181st Rifle Division
6. 147th Rifle Division
7. 196th Rifle Division
8. 28th Tank Corps
9. 214th Rifle Division

N

A pair of German 8.8cm dual-purpose Flak guns being moved into position during the fighting in the great bend of the Don. The German spearhead units were augmented with 8.8cm Flak guns to boost their anti-tank capability. In the open steppe terrain, the 8.8cm Flak gun could knock out T-34 tanks at ranges up to 2,000m. (Süddeutsche Zeitung, 00384631)

between two diverging axes of advance. The IV.Fliegerkorps would support Heeresgruppe A, while VIII.Fliegerkorps would support Heeresgruppe B's drive on Stalingrad. On a good day, the transport groups assigned to Luftflotte 4 could deliver about 200 tons of fuel to the front, which was barely sufficient to provide one VS each to two motorized divisions. Führer Directive No. 45 also switched most of Hoth's 4.Panzer-Armee back to supporting Heeresgruppe B's advance towards Stalingrad; Hoth assigned the 24.Panzer-Division to support Seydlitz-Kurzbach's LI.Armee-Korps against Chuikov's 64th Army. Furthermore, Hitler decided that the five divisions in Generaloberst Erich von Manstein's 11.Armee were not needed in the south and would proceed to Leningrad to mount an offensive by early September, thereby depriving the German forces in the south of any operational reserves.

Despite debilitating fuel shortages, von Wietersheim resumed his attack on 25 July with a daring flanking manoeuvre by elements of the 3. and 60.Infanterie divisions (mot.), which quickly rolled up Kolpakchi's right flank. The German motorized units advanced rapidly, reaching within 10km of Kalach by noon and encircling almost half of the 62nd Army. At the same time, LI.Armee-Korps (71. and 297.Infanterie divisions) and 24.Panzer-Division attacked those elements of Chuikov's 64th Army which were south of the Chir River. The 214th and 229th Rifle divisions were struck before their entire strength had reached the front, and they were forced back. Gordov recognized that Kolpakchi's 62nd Army was being enveloped, but he had limited resources of his own to mount a counter-stroke and was not authorized to retreat. Instead, he turned to Stavka for a solution. Stavka had just formed the 1st Tank Army near Stalingrad, under General-major Kirill S. Moskalenko. The 1st Tank Army was a powerful force, with about 525 tanks, and Stavka intended to use it in a major counter-offensive in conjunction with the still-forming 4th Tank Army in early August. Yet, alarmed by the sudden German breakthrough, Stavka suddenly agreed to release the 13th Tank Corps from 1st Tank Army so Gordov could mount an immediate counter-attack. Subsequently, Gordov committed two brigades from the 13th Tank

Corps across the Don, and they launched a furious counter-attack against Hube's 16.Panzer-Division in an effort to relieve the pressure on Kolpakchi. Once the Germans approached Kalach, Stavka agreed to allow the rest of 1st Tank Army as well as 4th Tank Army to be used to rescue 62nd Army. Gordov committed the 28th Tank Corps and 158th Tank Brigade against von Wietersheim's vanguard, dubbed Kampfgruppe Schlömer, which was nearly overrun by furious Soviet counter-attacks. Thus began one of the great tank battles of World War II, in the great bend of the Don.

On 26 July, Seydlitz-Kurzbach's LI.Armee-Korps and 24.Panzer-Division continued their attacks against Chuikov's off-balance 64th Army, and after 24 hours, managed not only to push it back to the Chir, but also to gain a toehold on the northern bank. Furthermore, LI.Armee-Korps pinned part of Chuikov's army (214th Rifle Division and 154th Naval Rifle Brigade) against the Don. Meanwhile, Gordov flung Moskalenko's 1st Tank Army against von Wietersheim's stranded XIV.Panzer-Korps with reckless abandon, but suffered heavy losses. By this point, the German vanguard was completely out of fuel and nearly out of ammunition – it was only sustained by Luftwaffe aerial resupply missions. If massed as a concentrated force, Moskalenko's 1st Tank Army had more than enough combat power to crush von Wietersheim's vanguard, but Gordov erred by feeding the 1st Tank Army into battle piecemeal, a few brigades at a time, which allowed the Germans to fend off each offensive jab. The Soviet 133rd Heavy Tank Brigade attacked without any prior reconnaissance, driving headlong at the Germans, and lost 28 of its 40 KV-1 tanks in a short action. In three days of fighting, Generalmajor Helmuth Schlömer's 3.Infanterie-Division (mot.) destroyed no fewer than 131 enemy tanks. Gordov upped the ante, adding in General-major Vasily D. Kriuchenkin's 4th Tank Army – the 22nd and 23rd Tank corps and 144th Heavy Tank Brigade. As with 1st Tank Army, 4th Tank Army was fed in piecemeal. Although outnumbered about 4:1 in armour, the Germans tipped the balance in their favour by concentrating VIII.Fliegerkorps to blunt the Soviet armoured attacks. Von Richthofen had moved up 80 Ju 87 Stukas from Sturzkampfgeschwader 2 to Tatsinskaya airbase, 150km to the south-west. On 26 and 27 July, there was intense aerial combat over the Don Bend, with 8th Air Army losing about 50 aircraft against about 25 for the Luftwaffe. The Italian 21st Group Caccia Terrestre was tasked with escorting the vulnerable Ju 87 Stukas, but lost at least four MC 200 fighters in this task. While the 8th Air Army managed to shoot down seven Stukas in three days, it could not prevent VIII. Fliegerkorps from mercilessly bombing the massed Soviet armour on the open steppes. Generaloberst Wolfram Freiherr von Richthofen also used his Bf 109E-7 fighter-bombers to attack enemy airstrips; on 27 July, one such raid destroyed 14 enemy fighters on the ground.

While Gordov's counter-offensive temporarily forced 6.Armee onto

German PzKpfw IV tanks, probably from 16.Panzer-Division, during the fighting in the great bend of the Don, mid-August 1942. The short-barrelled PzKpfw IV in the foreground appears to be a command vehicle. This region was near perfect tank terrain, and the weather allowed the Luftwaffe to bomb the enemy mercilessly. The Soviet decision to commit two tank armies, in piecemeal fashion, into this kind of battlefield was one of the great operational mistakes made during this long campaign. (Süddeutsche Zeitung, 00384540)

the defensive and prevented the annihilation of the 62nd Army, he had committed virtually all of the available Soviet armour into a chaotic battle of attrition. Due to their logistical problems, the Germans could not win the battle quickly, but their superior tactical skill, unit cohesion and air support allowed them to inflict punishing losses on Gordov's armour. By 28 July, 13th Tank Corps had succeeded in linking up with some of the encircled infantry (Group Zhuravlev) from the 62nd Army, and Hube's 16.Panzer-Division was under intense pressure. In the OKH, there was definite concern that Paulus' advance had been halted and faced disaster unless prompt resupply could be affected. Nevertheless, the Soviets frittered their tanks away in frontal assaults, while effective Luftwaffe close air support prevented any real success. By 31 July, the Soviets had lost about 611 tanks in the Don Bend, and both 1st Tank Army and 4th Tank Army were spent. In contrast, the Germans lost just 65 tanks destroyed in the Don Bend, although many more were damaged; the difference was that the Germans could usually recover their knocked-out tanks. Although hard-pressed, von Wietersheim's XIV. Panzer-Korps suffered 1,701 casualties from 21 to 31 July, including 330 dead or missing. Once it was clear that they would be unable to reach the encircled Group Zhuravlev, Gordov finally ordered the survivors to conduct a breakout; about 5,000 personnel succeeded in reaching Soviet lines, minus their heavy equipment.

Incensed by the failure to stop the German advance or to crush isolated units, Stalin issued his infamous Defence Order No. 227 ('*Ni Shagu Nazad*', or 'Not a step back!') on 28 July, demanding that the Red Army stop retreating. The NKVD began employing blocking detachments at key points, like bridges over the Don, to prevent unauthorized withdrawals, and commanders who retreated without authorization would face summary court martial. It was a draconian order, indicating the desperate nature of the Soviet military situation, only one month after the beginning of *Blau*. However, the Soviet leadership was unaware that the situation was not rosy on the other side either. On 30 July, Halder noted in his diary that, 'Sixth Army's striking power is paralyzed by ammunition and fuel supply difficulties'. Indeed, both Heeresgruppe A in the Caucasus and Heeresgruppe B in the Donbass were enfeebled by endemic fuel shortages. Such is the fog of war.

By early August, the fighting in the Don Bend had reached a stalemate, albeit a temporary one. The 1st Tank Army was so gutted that it was disbanded, and its remnants were simply absorbed into the 62nd Army. Dissatisfied with the course of the battle, Stalin decided once more on sweeping command changes. Kolpakchi was replaced by General-leytenant Anton I. Lopatin, who took over the embattled 62nd Army on 3 August. The next day, General-major Mikhail S. Shumilov took over the 64th Army from Chuikov, who became deputy army commander. On 4 August, General-polkovnik Andrei I. Eremenko arrived at Stalingrad and Stalin directed that the existing Stalingrad Front be split in two, with Gordov retaining command of the 21st, 62nd and 63rd armies and 4th Tank Army. Eremenko's new command was designated as the South-Eastern Front, and he gained control over the 1st Guards, 51st, 57th and 64th armies. Stalin's personnel changes added further confusion to an already strained Soviet command and control structure during a critical moment in the campaign, and ensured that the new commanders would not be familiar with their troops or the battlefield situation.

Hoth tries to outflank the Stalingrad Front, 31 July–9 August 1942

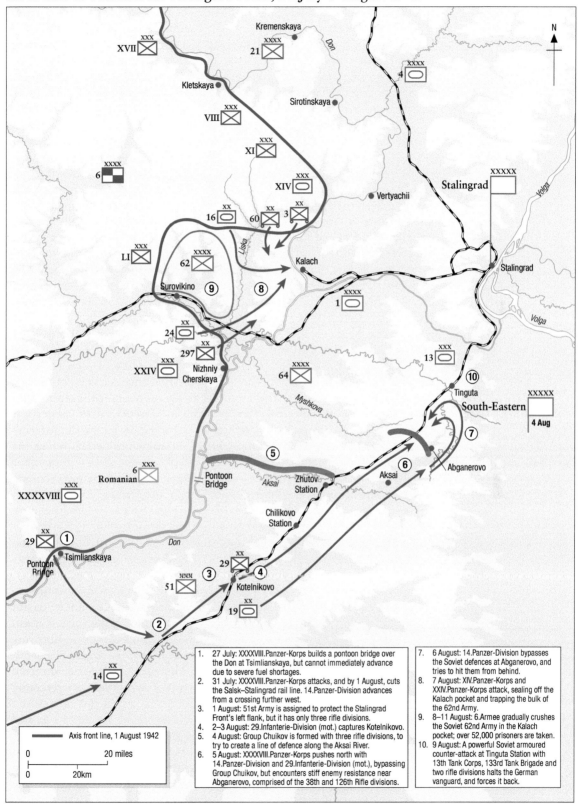

1. 27 July: XXXXVIII.Panzer-Korps builds a pontoon bridge over the Don at Tsimlianskaya, but cannot immediately advance due to severe fuel shortages.
2. 31 July: XXXXVIII.Panzer-Korps attacks, and by 1 August, cuts the Salsk–Stalingrad rail line. 14.Panzer-Division advances from a crossing further west.
3. 1 August: 51st Army is assigned to protect the Stalingrad Front's left flank, but it has only three rifle divisions.
4. 2–3 August: 29.Infanterie-Division (mot.) captures Kotelnikovo.
5. 4 August: Group Chuikov is formed with three rifle divisions, to try to create a line of defence along the Aksai River.
6. 5 August: XXXXVIII.Panzer-Korps pushes north with 14.Panzer-Division and 29.Infanterie-Division (mot.), bypassing Group Chuikov, but encounters stiff enemy resistance near Abganerovo, comprised of the 38th and 126th Rifle divisions.
7. 6 August: 14.Panzer-Division bypasses the Soviet defences at Abganerovo, and tries to hit them from behind.
8. 7 August: XIV.Panzer-Korps and XXIV.Panzer-Korps attack, sealing off the Kalach pocket and trapping the bulk of the 62nd Army.
9. 8–11 August: 6.Armee gradually crushes the Soviet 62nd Army in the Kalach pocket; over 52,000 prisoners are taken.
10. 9 August: A powerful Soviet armoured counter-attack at Tinguta Station with 13th Tank Corps, 133rd Tank Brigade and two rifle divisions halts the German vanguard, and forces it back.

ACROSS THE DON, 1–22 AUGUST 1942

Although much criticized by historians, Führer Directive No. 45 did help re-energize 6.Armee's drive on Stalingrad by providing immediate assistance from Hoth's 4.Panzer-Armee. Kempf's XXXXVIII.Panzer-Korps had already seized a crossing over the lower Don at Tsimlianskaya on 21 July, but could not immediately advance due to crippling fuel shortages. In the meantime, Kempf's *Pioniere* built a pontoon bridge over the Don and began slowly moving armour across the river. On 31 July, Kempf finally had received just enough fuel to attack, and he exploded out of the Tsimlianskaya bridgehead with 29.Infanterie-Division (mot.), followed by 14.Panzer-Division. At this point, General-major Trofim K. Kolomiets' 51st Army, which only had two rifle divisions (138th and 157th) deployed in this sector, could not stop Kempf's motorized units, which managed to sever the Salsk–Stalingrad rail line. Gordov ordered Kolomiets to protect the Stalingrad Front's left flank, but Kempf advanced rapidly, scattering Kolomiets' infantry and charging into Kotelnikovo on 2 August. The lead elements of the Soviet 208th Rifle Division had just arrived in Kotelnikovo by train and were stunned to be attacked by enemy armour while detraining, which resulted in four decimated battalions. The remnants of the 208th Rifle Division, along with two other battered divisions from the 51st Army, fell back in some disorder towards the Aksai River. Recognizing that someone needed to make a stand or his left flank would be wrecked, Gordov sent Chuikov to form a blocking force along the Aksai River using these three rifle divisions, plus the 6th Guards Tank Brigade and the 154th Naval Rifle Brigade. When General-major Shumilov took over the 64th Army, Group Chuikov was left as a semi-independent formation for the moment. In Moscow, Stavka reacted to the latest German advance by ordering the 35th and 36th Guards Airborne divisions to transfer to the Stalingrad Front, although they would not arrive for one week.

Chuikov rushed forwards to assume command of the blocking force, but Soviet command and control in the area south of the Aksai River had broken down. Gordov directed Khriukhin's 8th Air Army to attack Hoth's Panzers, even though the VVS had a poor track record in contributing to a mobile battle where the enemy's dispositions were unknown. Consequently, the VVS opted to attack fixed targets, assuming that the Germans were moving directly up the Salsk–Stalingrad rail line. In fact, it was the retreating 208th Rifle Division and other elements of the 51st Army that were retreating up the rail line, and they were mistakenly bombed at Chilikovo Station by the VVS on 4 August. Chuikov's own command post was bombed by Khriukhin's airmen and his only radio truck destroyed. Von Richthofen's Luftflotte 4 also bombed Group Chuikov, adding to its discomfiture.

Two German SPWs are being ferried across the Don at the Tsimlianskaya bridgehead, late July 1942. Initially, the Germans could only ferry across heavy equipment, but the *Pioneertruppen* were able to construct a pontoon bridge in a matter of days. (Author's collection)

In fact, Kempf was moving east of the Salsk–Stalingrad rail line in order to bypass enemy strongpoints, while the Romanian VI Corps screened his left flank. Although the Soviets were retreating in this sector, this was a high-risk manoeuvre, since Kempf's right flank was wide open and he had little information on the enemy forces ahead of him. Nevertheless, Kempf's XXXXVIII.Panzer-Korps advanced to the north-east, with 14.Panzer-Division and 29.Infanterie-Division (mot.), seizing a poorly guarded bridge over the Aksai and bypassing most of Chuikov's blocking force. However, pressing northwards on the morning of 5 August, the German vanguard encountered stiff enemy resistance near Abganerovo, comprised of the 38th and 126th Rifle divisions. The Soviet units had just arrived, but they were fortunate to occupy prepared defensive positions and to have some tank support, whereas the German vanguard only had a single company of tanks. Kempf reacted by ordering Generalmajor Ferdinand Heim's 14.Panzer-Division to swing around the Soviet defences at Abganerovo and hit them from behind. Heim succeeded in pushing between the two Soviet rifle divisions, but his division was nearly out of fuel. Furthermore, Soviet reinforcements were arriving, including the 13th Tank Corps. On 6 August, 14.Panzer-Division fended off numerous counter-attacks, claiming 51 enemy tanks destroyed, while the 29.Infanterie-Division (mot.) tried to envelop Abganerovo with a small *Kampfgruppe*. Instead, the Germans became involved in a tough tank battle on 7 August that lasted most of the day, and which cost them about a dozen tanks. Indeed, Kempf's position was increasingly precarious, since he failed to capture Abganerovo and his two motorized divisions were overextended in a salient and nearly out of fuel. Nor was the Romanian VI Corps capable of helping, beyond keeping Group Chuikov busy on the Aksai.

Romanian infantry pause, en route to the Don. Three infantry divisions from the Romanian VI Corps were assigned to support Hoth's crossing of the Don near Tsimlianskaya in late July 1942. Despite the addition of these forces, Hoth's right flank was wide open, with a *c.* 100km-wide gap between Heeresgruppe A and Heeresgruppe B. (Süddeutsche Zeitung, 00384551)

Meanwhile, the situation in the Don Bend had been deadlocked during the first week of August, with both sides content to bomb and shell the other, while preparing to make the next move. Paulus was finally able to gather enough fuel and ammunition to mount a major attack on the morning of 7 August. Hube's 16.Panzer-Division attacked from the north and achieved a breakthrough on the Liska River. The 24.Panzer-Division, attacking from the south, faced tough resistance, but also achieved a breakthrough. By nightfall, Lopatin's 62nd Army was in serious trouble and in danger of encirclement. Although the 62nd Army fought desperately to prevent the German pincers from closing, the Germans succeeded in completing the encirclement on 8 August. Gordov ordered the bridges over the Don destroyed before the Germans could capture them. Elements of 12 Soviet rifle divisions and ten tank brigades were encircled in the Kalach pocket, which the Germans moved quickly to eliminate. After three days of fighting, the 62nd Army was crushed, with 52,000 prisoners taken. Lopatin escaped, but was left with only 3,700 survivors from the 62nd Army to hold Kalach.

While Paulus was eliminating the Kalach pocket, Shumilov was preparing a major counter-attack with his 64th Army at Abganerovo. By the night of 8 August, he was able to amass three rifle divisions (38th, 126th and 204th) and 13th Tank Corps near Tinguta Station; it was not a particularly strong force, but Kempf was not expecting a major enemy attack. At dawn, Shumilov attacked, first with artillery, then infantry, supported by tanks. The Germans were hard-pressed and forced to withdraw 5km, as well as abandoning about a dozen damaged tanks. Although Shumilov's counterattack was unable to achieve more, it had accomplished its main goal of halting Kempf's advance towards Stalingrad from the south-east. Kempf was now forced to shift to the defensive, to await supplies and German infantry before he could resume his advance. In order to reinforce Kempf, Heeresgruppe B began transferring 24.Panzer-Division and IV.Armee-Korps with two infantry divisions (297. and 371.) across the Don.

Once the Kalach pocket had been crushed, Paulus moved to tidy up his front before pushing on towards Stalingrad. Kriuchenkin's 4th Tank Army had been stripped to only two rifle divisions (18th and 205th) and 22nd Tank Corps, but still held a substantial lodgement on the west side of the Don, north of Kalach. Paulus shifted most of his army 25km to his left, to achieve overwhelming mass against Kriuchenkin, while leaving only 71.Infanterie-Division to screen the Don between Kalach and Nizhniy Cherskaya. While Paulus was shifting his forces, Stalin decided to relieve Gordov of command (he became deputy front commander for the time being), and assigned Eremenko to command Stalingrad Front; Eremenko also retained command over the forces in the South-Eastern Front. Nikita Khrushchev served on the military council of both fronts, indicating a tacit recognition that Stalin's decision to split Stalingrad Front had not proved favourable.

On the morning of 15 August, Paulus attacked Kriuchenkin's 4th Tank Army with the bulk of his army in a mini-operation dubbed *Nord*, and quickly smashed the thin infantry screen. Von Wietersheim's XIV. Panzer-Korps reached the Don by the evening of 15 August, and occupied Sirotinskaya the next day. In response, elements of the 40th Guards Rifle Division hurriedly crossed the Don and tried to hold some of the high ground near Sirotinskaya, resulting in a famous action on Hill 180.9. According to Soviet accounts, a platoon from the 111th Guards Rifle Regiment under Leytenant Vasily D. Kochetkov sacrificed itself to hold off the German armour, knocking out six tanks. Kochetkov and five of his soldiers were posthumously awarded the Order of Lenin. Fighting continued for two more days around Hill 180.9, with the Soviets claiming to have inflicted substantial casualties upon the Germans. However, German records suggest that no tanks were lost in the fighting around Hill 180.9, and personnel losses were light. In any event, by 17 August, the Germans had overrun most of the Soviet bridgehead, except in the north around Kremenskaya. About 13,000 Soviet troops were captured as a result of Operation *Nord*. Eremenko rushed elements of General-major Kirill S. Moskalenko's 1st Guards Army to hold the Kremenskaya bridgehead; Moskalenko was unemployed after his 1st Tank Army was dissolved, and he was now given command of 1st Guards Army, formed from the 2nd Reserve Army. Two more Guards divisions – the 38th and 41st Guards Rifle divisions – joined the 40th Guards Rifle Division and managed to hold a perimeter just south of Kremenskaya. The German XI.Armee-Korps had two divisions outside the town, but could not overcome the Soviet resistance without tank support. However, Paulus was being pushed by the OKH to shift his armour to support his march on Stalingrad and did not want it tied up in a protracted mop-up action, so the Kremenskaya bridgehead remained in Soviet hands. Paulus probably believed that he could deal with the Kremenskaya bridgehead later, but this decision subsequently proved to be a serious mistake.

Pausing only briefly to regroup, Seydlitz-Kurzbach's LI.Armee-Korps assembled two infantry divisions (76. and 295.) along the Don, opposite Vertyachii. The river was about 250m wide in this sector, and it was near the operational boundary of the 62nd Army and the 4th Tank Army. The Soviets expected 6.Armee to try to cross the Don further south, near Kalach, and were caught by surprise by the German decision to cross at Vertyachii. Lopatin had deployed a fresh unit – General-major Josif F. Barinov's 98th Rifle Division (which arrived from the Far East only one week before) – in the Vertyachii–Peskovatka sector, but he kept his limited mobile reserves near Kalach. Before dawn on 21 August, the assault groups from four German regiments began crossing the Don in rafts and boats provided by Sturmboot-Kommando 902. Barinov's troops gave the Germans a hard time crossing the Don, shooting up 20 per cent of the watercraft and inflicting 425 casualties. Nevertheless, Seydlitz-Kurzbach's infantry succeeded in crossing the Don and establishing a bridgehead. Barinov's division was soon hard-pressed and one of its regiments surrounded. By late afternoon, 295.Infanterie-Division succeeded in building a 20-ton pontoon bridge at Luchenskiy, 3km west of Vertyachii. The 76.Infanterie-Division had more difficulty, but managed to complete a second pontoon bridge at Akimovskiy, by 0730hrs on 22 August. Paulus reinforced the bridgehead with two infantry divisions from Heitz's VIII.Armee-Korps (384. and 389.), but these units were met by fierce resistance from the 35th and 37th Guards Rifle divisions.

Lopatin sent what reinforcements he could towards Vertyachii, including part of the 87th Rifle Division and the understrength 40th Tank Brigade, while ordering the 35th Guards Rifle Division to build a second line of defence to contain any German breakout. Khriukhin's 8th Air Army mounted hundreds of sorties against the German pontoon bridges, but suffered crippling losses from enemy Flak and fighter interception. Indeed, 8th Air Army had lost so

German infantrymen cross the Don in inflatable boats. Given the lackadaisical attitude of the troops, sitting in the open, the crossing site does not appear to be threatened by enemy air or artillery attacks. Once the Germans were across the Don in strength, the advance to Stalingrad could begin forthwith. (Süddeutsche Zeitung, 00384490)

many aircraft in July and August that it was now outnumbered nearly 2:1 in the air. Consequently, 8th Air Army failed to prevent Luftwaffe bombers from mercilessly pounding Soviet reserve units marching towards the front. At this critical moment, von Richthofen's Luftflotte 4 controlled the skies over the battlefield. Seydlitz-Kurzbach expanded his bridgehead at Vertyachii, and during 22 August, Hube's 16.Panzer-Division and 3.Infanterie-Division (mot.) began crossing the Don bridges and assembling on the eastern bank; Hube's division had 83 operational tanks and Schlömer's division had 42 tanks. On the same day, Moskalenko's 1st Guards Army launched a daring counter-attack with his three Guards Rifle divisions against XI.Armee-Korps, from the Kremenskaya bridgehead. Slowly, Moskalenko's troops began forcing XI.Armee-Korps to give some ground, although Paulus paid this little heed. German attention was now firmly fixed on initiating the endgame at Stalingrad.

Further south, Hoth had resumed his offensive against Shumilov's 64th Army on 20 August, gaining some ground with 14. and 24.Panzer divisions north-east of Abganerovo. However, Soviet resistance in this sector was very strong and Hoth could not achieve a breakthrough. Furthermore, Eremenko had deployed the 57th Army around Lake Sarpa, to try to prevent Hoth from making any wide flanking movements to envelop Shumilov's line. Nevertheless, 24.Panzer-Division succeeded on 21 and 22 August in outflanking the 64th Army before the 57th Army was fully prepared. Shumilov proved to be a steady commander and did not panic; instead, he scraped together his limited reserves and dug in, forcing Hoth into a tough fight around Tinguta Station. The 208th Rifle Division, still in the line, was left with only 502 men and no artillery.

The retreating Red Army demolished the railroad bridge at Kalach over the Don on 8 August, after the destruction of the encircled 62nd Army units west of the river. The Germans were unable to repair the bridge for months, and relied upon trucks and captured Soviet trains to ferry supplies forwards to 6.Armee at Stalingrad. Kalach became the main supply base of 6.Armee during the next several months. (Bundesarchiv, Bild 255-014, Foto: Thalheim)

6.Armee closes in on Stalingrad, 12–29 August 1942

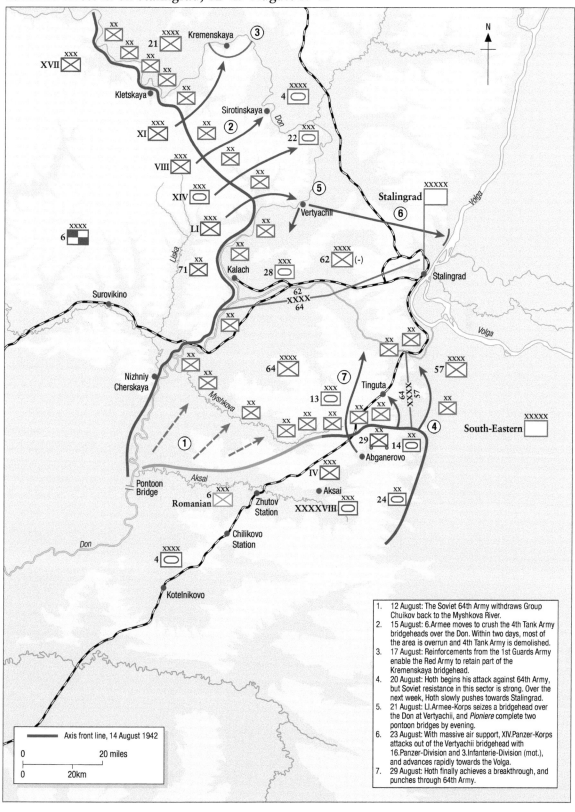

1. 12 August: The Soviet 64th Army withdraws Group Chuikov back to the Myshkova River.
2. 15 August: 6.Armee moves to crush the 4th Tank Army bridgeheads over the Don. Within two days, most of the area is overrun and 4th Tank Army is demolished.
3. 17 August: Reinforcements from the 1st Guards Army enable the Red Army to retain part of the Kremenskaya bridgehead.
4. 20 August: Hoth begins his attack against 64th Army, but Soviet resistance in this sector is strong. Over the next week, Hoth slowly pushes towards Stalingrad.
5. 21 August: LI.Armee-Korps seizes a bridgehead over the Don at Vertyachii, and *Pioniere* complete two pontoon bridges by evening.
6. 23 August: With massive air support, XIV.Panzer-Korps attacks out of the Vertyachii bridgehead with 16.Panzer-Division and 3.Infanterie-Division (mot.), and advances rapidly towards the Volga.
7. 29 August: Hoth finally achieves a breakthrough, and punches through 64th Army.

At this point, Paulus' operational intent was to conduct a double pincer attack against the Stalingrad Front, with von Wietersheim's XIV.Panzer-Korps leading the northern pincer and Kempf's XXXXVIII.Panzer-Korps leading the southern pincer. The 62nd and 64th armies would be caught within the jaws of these pincers, which would then lead to the rapid fall of Stalingrad and the successful conclusion of the campaign. However, the stiff resistance of the 64th Army derailed Paulus' plan by delaying Hoth's advance from the south.

TO THE VOLGA, 23 AUGUST–3 SEPTEMBER 1942

At 0445hrs on 23 August, von Wietersheim's XIV.Panzer-Korps began its breakout from the Vertyachii bridgehead, preceded by an aerial blitz. The VIII.Fliegerkorps put in a maximum effort, first using its fighters to clear the skies over the battlefield and then using its Stukas and bombers to blast any sign of resistance in front of Hube's on-rushing 16.Panzer-Division. Barinov's 98th Rifle Division was quickly smashed, with only 700 of its troops escaping to Stalingrad. Emerging from the bridgehead, Hube deployed his division into two regimental-size *Kampfgruppen* (Sieckenius and von Strachwitz) and boldly advanced eastwards in great clouds of dust. Hauptmann Johannes Steinhoff, commander of II./Jagdgeschwader 52, wrote that, 'we flew at low level above the roads on which our troops advanced. Everywhere the soldiers on the ground acted crazy with joy. The summer was dry and as we flew over the spearheads, the dust clouds from the tank formations reached high above the ground into the clear sky.'

Eremenko ordered Khriukhin's 8th Air Army to commit everything to stop the German drive, even biplane night-bombers. Even the obsolescent I-16 and I-153 fighters from Stalingrad's air defence unit, the 102nd Fighter Aviation Division PVO, were committed. However, the uncoordinated Soviet air units were simply slaughtered by VIII.Fliegerkorps' fighters, who claimed

An SdKfz 231 (8-rad) armoured car from 16.Panzer-Division was one of the first vehicles to reach the banks of the Volga on the evening of 23 August 1942. The Soviets were surprised by the sudden German lunge towards the river, and had to rush units to defend northern Stalingrad. Although the Germans did not yet know it, this proved to be the high-water mark of the Third Reich. (Bundesarchiv, RH 20-6 Bild-00216-017)

Stalingrad and the Volga, seen from the east. At first glance, the city seemed nearly empty, and 6.Armee appeared to be within easy reach of achieving its final objective. (Author's collection)

over 60 victories on this day. Soviet fighters only managed to shoot down two German aircraft, a Stuka and an He 111. Six other German aircraft were lost to Soviet anti-aircraft fire. Due to the Luftwaffe's control of the airspace over the battlefield, Eremenko was deprived of aerial reconnaissance and was unaware of the extent of the German breakthrough. Consequently, there was no coordinated response to the German advance. The 35th Guards Rifle Division, which Lopatin's 62nd Army had ordered to develop a second line of defence, mounted a local counter-attack against 3.Infanterie-Division (mot.) with a single rifle battalion and 16 T-34 tanks from the 169th Tank Brigade led by Hero of the Soviet Union Kapitan Pavel A. Semenov. Although some losses were inflicted, this puny counter-attack was simply brushed aside, and Semenov was mortally wounded. By early afternoon, Hube's spearhead had advanced over 30km and the outskirts of northern Stalingrad were on the horizon.

German infantry from XIV. Panzer-Korps begin attacking into the northern suburb of Rynok in late August. The Soviets were able to reinforce this sector just in time, leading to a protracted battle. (Author's collection)

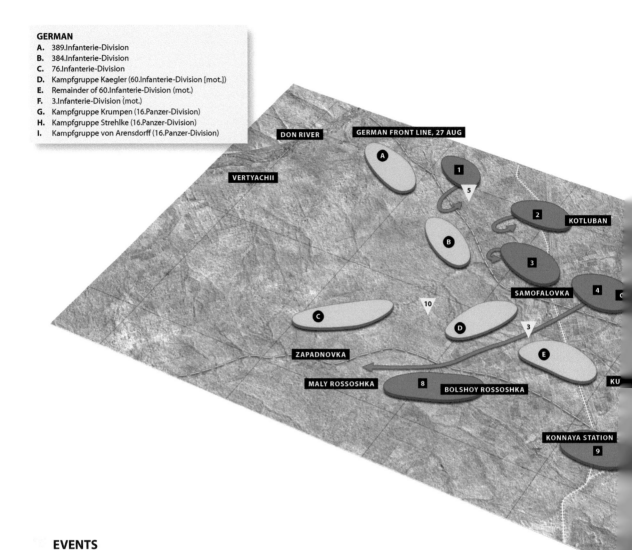

GERMAN

- A. 389.Infanterie-Division
- B. 384.Infanterie-Division
- C. 76.Infanterie-Division
- D. Kampfgruppe Kaegler (60.Infanterie-Division [mot.])
- E. Remainder of 60.Infanterie-Division (mot.)
- F. 3.Infanterie-Division (mot.)
- G. Kampfgruppe Krumpen (16.Panzer-Division)
- H. Kampfgruppe Strehlke (16.Panzer-Division)
- I. Kampfgruppe von Arensdorff (16.Panzer-Division)

DON RIVER

GERMAN FRONT LINE, 27 AUG

VERTYACHII

KOTLUBAN

SAMOFALOVKA

ZAPADNOVKA

MALY ROSSOSHKA

BOLSHOY ROSSOSHKA

KU

KONNAYA STATION

EVENTS

1. 23 August, 1835hrs: Lead elements of 16.Panzer-Division reach the Volga north of Rynok. One company moves into Spartanovka.

2. 23 August: Eremenko orders reinforcements to defend northern Stalingrad, including 10th NKVD Division, 28th Naval Infantry Brigade and 99th Tank Brigade.

3. Night, 23 August: The Soviet 35th Guards Rifle Division and 169th Tank Brigade, attacking from the north, sever XIV.Panzer-Korps' lines of communication.

4. 24 August: XIV.Panzer-Korps assumes hedgehog positions to defend its gains. The Luftwaffe provides limited aerial resupply.

5. 24 August: The 4th Tank Army makes repeated attacks against the Vertyachii bridgehead, but is repeatedly repulsed.

6. 24 August: Eremenko forms two shock groups to completely sever the German corridor to the Volga. Group Shtevnev attacks from the south, and manages to push 16.Panzer-Division out of Orlovka. Group Kovalenko begins attacking from the north, but its initial attacks are repulsed.

7. 26 August: Both Group Kovalenko and Group Shtevnev launch a powerful, coordinated dawn assault. The 4th and 16th Tank corps fail to budge 3.Infanterie-Division (mot.), and lose 224 of 340 tanks in two days of fighting.

8. 27 August: Attacks by 23rd Tank Corps near Konnaya Station are repulsed with the loss of 15 tanks.

9. 28–29 August: Group Kovalenko continues to attack the northern front, but all efforts are repulsed.

10. 29–30 August: The 6.Armee re-establishes direct contact with XIV.Panzer-Korps.

11. 31 August: Still under heavy pressure, Hube's 16.Panzer-Division abandons Rynok, and pulls back 2km.

XIV xxx

VON WEITERSHEIM

LI xxx

VON SEYDLITZ

XIV.PANZER-KORPS FIGHTS FOR ITS LIFE, 23–31 AUGUST 1942

The arrival of XIV.Panzer-Korps at the western bank of the Volga, near the northern suburbs of Stalingrad, was a dramatic event that heralded an imminent German victory. However, the Germans only succeeded in driving a very narrow corridor through Soviet lines to the river, and the Stalingrad Front reacted violently to this incursion. As a result, XIV.Panzer-Korps was cut off, and forced to spend a desperate week-long battle trying to avoid being crushed by Soviet counter-attacks.

KOVALENKO   SHTEVNEV

62

LOPATIN

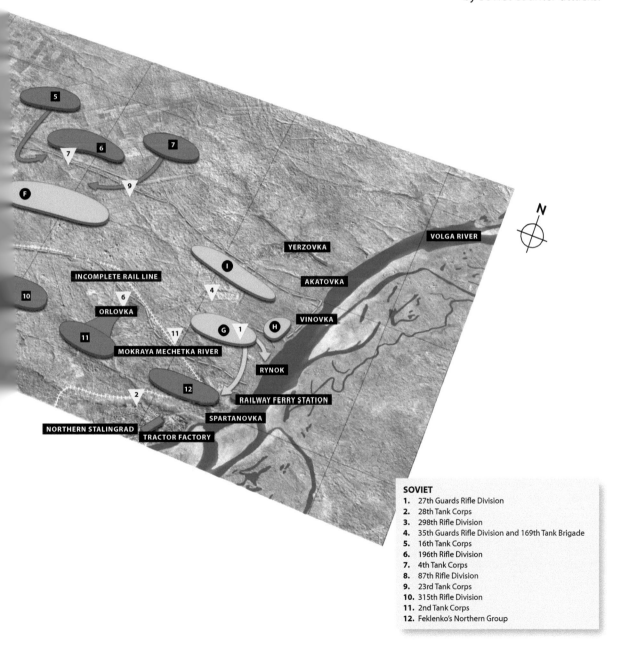

VOLGA RIVER

YERZOVKA

AKATOVKA

INCOMPLETE RAIL LINE

ORLOVKA

VINOVKA

MOKRAYA MECHETKA RIVER

RYNOK

RAILWAY FERRY STATION

SPARTANOVKA

NORTHERN STALINGRAD

TRACTOR FACTORY

SOVIET
1. 27th Guards Rifle Division
2. 28th Tank Corps
3. 298th Rifle Division
4. 35th Guards Rifle Division and 169th Tank Brigade
5. 16th Tank Corps
6. 196th Rifle Division
7. 4th Tank Corps
8. 87th Rifle Division
9. 23rd Tank Corps
10. 315th Rifle Division
11. 2nd Tank Corps
12. Feklenko's Northern Group

An aerial view of Stalingrad after being set ablaze by von Richthofen's bombers, 23–24 August 1942. Luftwaffe attacks proved counter-productive: the rubble-strewn streets limited German mobility, and the ruined buildings made excellent fortresses for the defenders. (Author's collection)

The sudden German breakthrough caught the Soviets off guard, and Eremenko had no significant units immediately at hand in this sector, even if he had been aware that German armour was approaching the city. Instead, Hube quickly discovered that only worker militia units and anti-aircraft units defended the northern part of Stalingrad. Soviet civilians and soldiers alike were stunned to see German tanks suddenly approaching the city outskirts. The 1077th Anti-Aircraft Regiment had five batteries equipped with 85mm (52-K) M1939 guns deployed in the vicinity of Orlovka, and they were ordered to lower their barrels and engage Hube's armour. The Soviet anti-aircraft gunners began engaging the German tanks at a range of about 700m, although they had no armour-piercing rounds and the troops were not even equipped with small arms. According to Soviet accounts, the 1077th Anti-Aircraft Regiment knocked out 83 enemy tanks and destroyed three battalions of motorized infantry, while admitting the loss of 354 personnel (including 46 females). According to German accounts, no tanks were lost in this action, and German losses were minimal, while 37 AA guns were destroyed. In all likelihood, some German tanks were knocked out by the Soviet anti-aircraft crews, but it is also apparent that the nearly defenceless batteries were quickly overrun. In any event, around 1835hrs, reconnaissance units from Hube's 16.Panzer-Division reached the Volga north of the suburb of Rynok, and were astounded to see both the wide river and the endless steppes beyond. Hube's division had advanced nearly 60km in 14 hours.

Ju 87 Stuka dive-bombers over northern Stalingrad. Von Richthofen's Luftflotte 4 tried to smash resistance in the city to assist 6.Armee's advance, but the damage inflicted on Red Army units in the city was modest. Instead, German infantrymen would have to root out the defenders, block by block. (Author's collection)

While ordering some of his division to begin digging in, Hube decided to launch probing attacks into the city's northern suburbs to gauge enemy resistance. One battalion from Grenadier-Regiment 79 occupied Rynok and the railway ferry station on the Volga, while a single company from Grenadier-Regiment 64 moved into Spartanovka. Hube's troops were less than 3km from the Stalingrad Tractor Works (Stalingradski Traktorni Zavod, STZ) and Soviet resistance was minimal, but the Germans were reluctant to push into a major city, late in the day, with tired troops. Instead, von Richthofen deployed VIII.Fliegerkorps to conduct a massive terror bombing of Stalingrad, hoping to disrupt Soviet defensive efforts and undermine the enemy's morale. In a steady stream, the German bombers appeared over the city and proceeded to dump about 1,000 tons of bombs, setting large sections of the city ablaze. Soviet anti-aircraft fire was ineffective, shooting down only a single enemy bomber. The bombing and subsequent conflagration caused thousands of civilian casualties in the city – Soviet sources claim up to 40,000 dead or wounded from a prewar population of 445,000 – and began the process of destruction that would gradually reduce Stalingrad into a pile of charred rubble.

Belatedly learning about Hube's advance, Eremenko ordered reinforcements sent at once to block Hube from getting into northern Stalingrad – but not much was available. Polkovnik Aleksandr A. Saraev, commander of the 10th NKVD Division, had been made garrison commander of Stalingrad, but his division was scattered across the 62nd Army area and he could only send the 282nd Rifle Regiment (NKVD) to defend the Tractor

A Soviet 37mm (61-K) anti-aircraft battery, on a rooftop in Stalingrad, scans the skies. The Air Defence Command (PVO) of Stalingrad was based on seven medium anti-aircraft regiments and a variety of smaller detachments, but it was overwhelmed by the massive Luftwaffe raids on 23 and 24 August, which set Stalingrad ablaze. Most of the gun crews were very young, and 60 per cent were female. Only a single German aircraft was lost to anti-aircraft fire in the first 200-bomber raid. (Author's collection)

Works. Aside from about 1,000 poorly armed Stalingrad militiamen, the only other unit immediately available was the 32nd Battalion from the Volga Flotilla, with 220 naval infantrymen. A few anti-tank and artillery batteries were formed from personnel at hand, in order to stiffen the defence. General-major Nikolai V. Feklenko, now in charge of the Stalingrad armour training centre located near the STZ, took command of the reinforcements formed into the so-called 'northern group'. Feklenko brought the 21st Tank Training Battalion (which possessed 30 T-34 tanks) into action, and it was placed under the 99th Tank Brigade headquarters. The STZ also provided a number of repaired T-34 and KV-1 tanks to Feklenko, as well. Eremenko promised more reinforcements, but Feklenko would have only a few battalions to defend northern Stalingrad for the next several days.

Although von Wietersheim's XIV.Panzer-Korps had succeeded in breaking through to the Volga and the Stalingrad suburbs, the corps was now strung out defending a very vulnerable 50km-long corridor. Even worse, Hube's 16.Panzer-Division had expended most of its fuel just to reach the Volga and now had very little left. The bulk of Paulus' 6.Armee was still involved in the bridgehead battle around Vertyachii, meaning that no infantry would be immediately available to relieve von Wietersheim's XIV.Panzer-Korps. The 60.Infanterie-Division (mot.) was sent forwards from the bridgehead to link up with the two stranded German motorized divisions, but was only able to affect a tenuous contact. Eremenko was quick to recognize the German predicament, and ordered Lopatin's 62nd Army and Kriuchenkin's 4th Tank Army to launch counter-attacks to sever the narrow enemy corridor. At this

In the wake of 6.Armee's advance, German support units were obliged to repair bridges and rail lines in order to create a viable line of communications to support Paulus' army. Civilians from Organization Todt and captured Soviet volunteers (Hiwis) helped, but much of the work was done by various construction units under Heeresgruppe B. (Nik Cornish@www.stavka.org)

A German PzKpfw III tank and infantry pause, on the outskirts of Stalingrad. The 6.Armee's vanguard reached Stalingrad with insufficient strength to seize the city in a coup de main, as occurred at Voronezh, and was forced to wait for reinforcements to arrive before beginning a major push into the city. (Süddeutsche Zeitung, 00384621)

moment, the availability of a strong mobile reserve, like 1st Tank Army, could have proved decisive, but this formation had been squandered in the Don Bend fighting. Eremenko was left with only bits and pieces of decimated tank corps to mount counter-attacks. Nevertheless, the 35th Guards Rifle Division and 169th Tank Brigade were able to mount a significant attack on the evening of 23/24 August, which cut across the German corridor and temporarily severed von Wietersheim's line of communications.

Von Wietersheim ordered his three divisions to adopt hedgehog defensive positions, in order to ward off the expected Soviet counter-attacks. He also requested that the Luftwaffe provide aerial resupply of fuel and ammunition to his isolated corps, although only token amounts could be delivered so close to the front. Kriuchenkin's 4th Tank Army began launching strong attacks against the Vertyachii bridgehead on 24 August, but was repeatedly repulsed by VIII.Armee-Korps' stubborn defence. Paulus slowly expanded the Vertyachii bridgehead, pushing back the 62nd Army's threadbare divisions. Eremenko recognized that the Germans were attempting a double pincer attack against the Stalingrad Front, and he had to judiciously decide where to commit his limited reinforcements. Although the 62nd Army was in desperate straits, he also had to provide the 57th and 64th armies with enough forces to prevent Hoth from breaking through in the south. Stavka RVGK still had plentiful reserves, but von Wietersheim's advance now blocked the direct rail line to Stalingrad, and the Luftwaffe made traffic on the Volga difficult, which meant it took longer for units to reach the front.

Eremenko probably would have preferred to wait for more reinforcements to arrive before launching a counter-attack, but Stalin called him on the morning of 24 August and ordered him to immediately close the German corridor to the Volga. As a result, Eremenko directed the formation of two shock groups to attack XIV.Panzer-Korps' corridor to the Volga forthwith. On the northern flank, Group Kovalenko was formed under General-major Kirill A. Kovalenko, deputy commander of the Stalingrad Front, and directed to attack south from the Samofalovka–Kotluban sector. Initially, Kovalenko had just two rifle divisions and the 28th Tank Corps, which attacked the

German assault guns, possibly from Sturmgeschütz-Abteilung 177, probe the outer northern outskirts of Stalingrad, late August 1942. German AFVs could be effective in the suburbs, but once they moved into the inner city, rubbled streets limited their mobility. (Bundesarchiv, Bild 183-B22414)

base of the corridor on 24 August, but were repulsed. Kovalenko's 35th Guards Rifle Division had briefly severed the German corridor, but these forces were soon mopped up by 60.Infanterie-Division (mot.), which moved east from the Vertyachii bridgehead. In the south, the 62nd Army formed Group Shtevnev under General-leytenant Andrei D. Shtevnev, a tanker. Shtevnev assembled the 2nd and 23rd Tank corps and managed to push Hube's troops out of Orlovka, but was not yet capable of conducting a larger effort against the corridor. Schlömer's 3.Infanterie-Division (mot.), holding the centre of the corridor, was able to fend off attacks from both north and south and maintain a connection with Hube's 16.Panzer-Division. The VIII. Fliegerkorps not only continued to bomb Stalingrad, but also conducted multiple air strikes against Soviet troop concentrations on either side of the corridor, which hindered the ability of either shock group to mount a powerful attack.

Nevertheless, Hube's 16.Panzer-Division was in a desperate state, with minimal supplies of ammunition and fuel remaining. On the night of 24 August, Hube told his staff that, 'I absolutely refuse to fight a pointless battle that must end in the annihilation of my troops and I therefore order a breakout to the west. I shall personally take responsibility for this order.' However, before Hube ordered the breakout, the Soviet attacks on the corridor ceased, and a small amount of supplies reached his isolated division. Hube decided to hang on and await rescue. It took two days for Kovalenko and Shtevnev to organize a more powerful, coordinated attack, during which time the German situation in the corridor slightly improved. On the morning of 26 August, both Soviet shock groups attacked the corridor. In the north, Kovalenko tried to punch through Schlömer's 3.Infanterie-Division (mot.) with the 4th and 16th Tank corps east of Kuzmichi, but attacking in broad daylight across open terrain proved disastrous. The German hedgehogs were vulnerable to artillery, but the Soviets had very little artillery support in these sectors. Instead, the German 8.8cm Flak guns and 7.5cm anti-tank guns ripped apart the advancing Soviet armour, knocking out 224 of the 340 tanks committed. In the south, Shtevnev attacked with the 2nd and 23rd Tank corps near Konnaya Station, but was also repulsed with heavy losses. Both Soviet shock groups continued to attack between 27 and 29 August, without ever achieving a link-up between the two groups. Although the Soviet formations had enjoyed a significant numerical superiority, they were poorly coordinated, and attacked under conditions that were most favorable for the enemy's anti-tank tactics.

The only real Soviet success achieved during this period was by Feklenko's northern group, which managed to push the 16.Panzer-Division out of Spartanovka and created a solid defensive line along the Mokraya Mechetka. Feklenko also received reinforcements. During the night of 27/28 August, Polkovnik Sergei F. Gorokhov's 124th Rifle Brigade was ferried across the Volga, followed on the next night by the 149th Rifle Brigade. Gorokhov was put in charge of the northern group, which now became Group Gorokhov; this grouping became the bedrock of the Soviet defence in the northern part of the city.

During Eremenko's brief counter-offensive, Seydlitz-Kurzbach mounted a surprise assault crossing of the Don at Kalach with the 71.Infanterie-Division on the night of 24/25 August. Lopatin's 62nd Army had shifted most of its forces to support the counter-attack on the corridor, and left only depleted units to guard Kalach. Stunned by the German crossing, the 62nd Army pulled back 5km from the Don, which emboldened Seydlitz-Kurzbach to launch a major attack with two divisions (76. and 295.) south from the Vertyachii bridgehead on the morning of 26 August. Recognizing that 62nd Army's centre had been pierced, Lopatin pleaded to be allowed to withdraw to the Rossoshka River – which Eremenko grudgingly authorized. The withdrawal of Lopatin's 62nd Army eased some of the pressure on the south side of the corridor and also increased the vulnerability of Shumilov's 64th Army in the south.

On the *Rollbahn* (military highway) heading to Stalingrad. Note that a large part of the German logistic columns consists of horse-drawn carts. The 6.Armee was operating at the end of an extremely long and fragile supply line, which had very limited throughput. Consequently, German logistic shortfalls would make an all-out effort at Stalingrad difficult until rail supply was feasible. (Bundesarchiv, Bild 169-0241)

Kempf's XXXXVIII.Panzer-Korps had been briefly fought to a standstill by 25 August, when they encountered prepared defences on hills west of Lake Sarpa. Soviet artillery fire and dug-in tanks from the 57th Army inflicted heavy personnel and materiel losses on 24.Panzer-Division, which halted Kempf's advance. Recognizing that the Soviet defences in this sector were too strong, Hoth decided to look for another approach. German reconnaissance suggested that Shumilov had strengthened his left flank, at the expense of his centre. Demonstrating agility, between 26 and 28 August Hoth quietly shifted the three mechanized divisions of Kempf's XXXXVIII.Panzer-Korps 35km to the south-west, near Abganerovo Station, while replacing them with two infantry divisions (94. and 371.) from IV.Armee-Korps. Shumilov did not detect the movement of Kempf's armour to the west. Hoth further obfuscated his manoeuvre by leaving the Romanian 2nd and 20th Infantry divisions in place, in the sector chosen for the next attack; the Romanian positions along the Myshkova River had formed a quiet sector for weeks. On the morning of 29 August, Kempf's corps conducted a forward passage of lines through the Romanian units in order to strike Shumilov's centre. The 24.Panzer-Division overran the Soviet 126th Rifle Division, while 14.Panzer-Division overwhelmed the 29th Rifle Division. Both Soviet divisions were smashed, enabling Kempf to advance 18km on the first day. Shumilov's centre was pierced, and a large portion of the 64th Army was in danger of encirclement. Although Eremenko was against yielding any ground – in accordance with Stalin's 'no retreat' order – he recognized that Hoth's breakthrough could lead to the annihilation of the 62nd and 64th armies; if that occurred, Stalingrad could not be held. On 30 August, Eremenko ordered a general withdrawal, with Shumilov's right wing and broken centre to regroup behind the Chervlenaia River. The rest of Lopatin's 62nd Army would retreat from the Don and fall in behind the Rossoshka. At the same time, on 30 August, 6.Armee finally re-established ground lines of communications with von Wietersheim's XIV.Panzer-Korps, thereby ending the crisis.

Eremenko's hopes for creating a new defensive line with the 62nd and 64th armies behind the Chervlenaia and Rossoshka rivers proved futile. The 24.Panzer-Division vaulted forwards on 31 August, crossing the Chervlenaia River before the retreating Soviet units could establish a new line. On the same day, Seydlitz-Kurzbach's LI.Armee-Korps began crossing the Rossoshka, pushing back the 62nd Army. At this point, the Germans were extremely close to encircling a large portion of the 62nd and 64th armies, but made a serious tactical mistake. Instead of ordering 24.Panzer-Division to push north to link up with Seydlitz-Kurzbach's infantry, Hoth ordered that division to try to push directly towards Stalingrad. On 1 September, 24.Panzer-Division advanced towards Stalingrad, but was stopped outside the western approaches to the city by the 20th Tank Destroyer Brigade. Paulus also failed to recognize his window of opportunity to cut off the retreating Soviet armies, and failed to press Seydlitz-Kurzbach to advance faster. As a result of these German tactical errors, the bulk of the 62nd and 64th armies were able to evade encirclement and withdraw to the western outskirts of Stalingrad, where they established a new line. On the afternoon of 2 September, LI.Armee-Korps finally linked up with the Romanian 20th Infantry Division, creating a continuous front between Hoth's and Paulus' forces.

Although the Soviet armies had been battered and Eremenko's reserves were minimal, Paulus and Hoth lacked the strength to mount an immediate attack into Stalingrad. The German logistical situation was still extremely tenuous, and the units that had led the advance to the city were exhausted after weeks of continuous combat. The 24.Panzer-Division had only one-quarter of its authorized number of tanks still operational, and the other mechanized units averaged 30–50 per cent of their armour. Paulus opted for a methodical approach: bring up infantry reserves, repair damaged vehicles, deploy artillery, resupply and then, once 6.Armee's strength was restored, launch a powerful, coordinated attack into the city. For once, both Hitler and the OKH were satisfied with progress at Stalingrad, and allowed Paulus some leeway to regroup. Under normal conditions, Eremenko might have enjoyed a brief respite to reorganize the city's defences and prepare for the next round, but this was not the case. Instead, Eremenko's situation was complicated by the arrival of Zhukov from Moscow on 29 August. Zhukov had the authority of a senior Stavka representative, and immediately pressured Eremenko to renew his counter-offensive against the XIV.Panzer-Korps corridor, even though the last offensive had just ended in a costly fiasco. Zhukov gave Eremenko orders to conduct another major counter-offensive within a matter of days, which completely ignored the actual situation on the ground.

THE VITAL FLANKS

While the main action was occurring on the Stalingrad axis, important events were occurring on both flanks that would influence the ultimate outcome of the campaign. In the Caucasus, Heeresgruppe A initially made good progress and captured its first objective, the Maikop oilfields, on 10 August. Soviet resistance was strong in a few places, but the enemy lacked the armoured

Both the Italian and Hungarian divisions relied upon elderly 10cm howitzers for their primary fire support. These weapons had inadequate range by the standards of 1942, and their wooden wheels and horse-drawn transport made them slow to employ on the battlefield. (Nik Cornish@www.stavka.org)

Soviet counter-offensive against left flank of 6.Armee, 20–28 August 1942

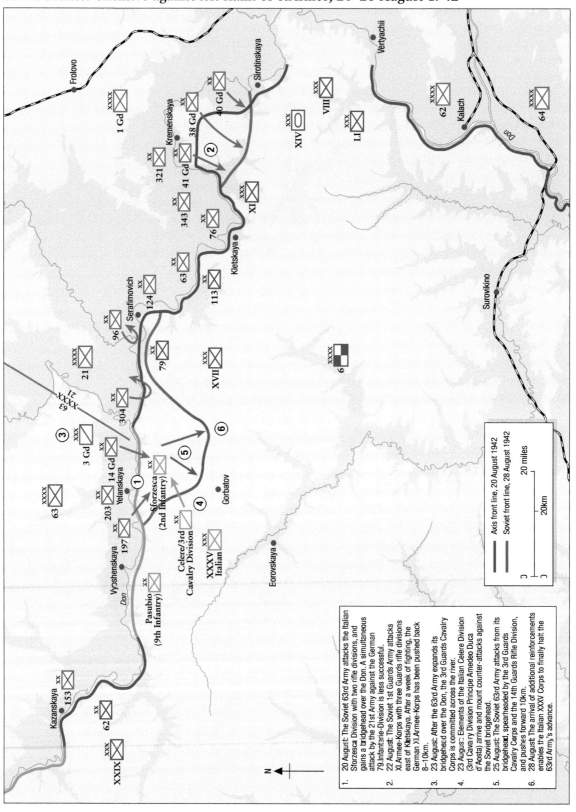

1. 20 August: The Soviet 63rd Army attacks the Italian Sforzesca Division with two rifle divisions, and gains a bridgehead over the Don. A simultaneous attack by the 21st Army against the German 79.Infanterie-Division is less successful.

2. 22 August: The Soviet 1st Guards Army attacks XI.Armee-Korps with three Guards rifle divisions east of Kletskaya. After a week of fighting, the German XI.Armee-Korps has been pushed back 8–10km.

3. 23 August: After the 63rd Army expands its bridgehead over the Don, the 3rd Guards Cavalry Corps is committed across the river.

4. 23 August: Elements of the Italian Celere Division (3rd Cavalry Division Principe Amedeo Duca d'Aosta) arrive and mount counter-attacks against the Soviet bridgehead.

5. 25 August: The Soviet 63rd Army attacks from its bridgehead, spearheaded by the 3rd Guards Cavalry Corps and the 14th Guards Rifle Division, and pushes forward 10km.

6. 28 August: The arrival of additional reinforcements enables the Italian XXXV Corps to finally halt the 63rd Army's advance.

Axis front line, 20 August 1942

Soviet front line, 28 August 1942

20 miles

20km

N

reserves to launch powerful counter-attacks. However, logistic problems plagued the German advance into the Caucasus even more than it did the advance to Stalingrad, due to the greater distances involved. Heeresgruppe A's efforts were also split between advancing towards the remaining oilfields and overrunning the Black Sea ports, which led to a dispersal of forces. By the end of August, the German invasion of the Caucasus was still proceeding, but was suffering from overextension, which made it unclear if it could accomplish its objectives. Furthermore, there was a huge gap between Heeresgruppe A's left flank and Heeresgruppe B's right flank, which was screened by only a single division – 16.Infanterie-Division (mot.). Rather than the complementary operations envisioned in the *Blau* plan, the two German army groups were no longer even within supporting range of each other.

Once Heeresgruppe B succeeded in reaching the Volga, von Weichs was now obliged to hold a front that was more than 700km in length, stretching all the way back to Voronezh. The 2.Armee had built a solid defence around Voronezh, but it was under continuous attack by the Bryansk and Voronezh fronts. Stavka believed that operations in the Voronezh sector would force Heeresgruppe B to divert forces away from Stalingrad. After the failure of the 5th Tank Army's counter-offensive, Stavka directed the Bryansk Front to launch another major operation in late July. Group Chibisov, comprising four tank corps, was committed against the sector held by the German VII.Armee-Korps north-west of Voronezh. Vatutin's Voronezh Front was also ordered to launch major attacks by the 40th and 60th armies against the right flank of VII.Armee-Korps, as well. Chibisov was able to breach the German front on 21 July and advance 21km. Vatutin also achieved limited success, pushing into the northern suburbs of Voronezh with repeated infantry attacks. However, Salmuth's 2.Armee was able to mount a well-timed counter-attack by the 9.Panzer-Division, which caved in Chibisov's flank. General-major Aleksandr I. Liziukov, the former commander of 5th Tank Army but now only in command of 2nd Tank Corps, was killed trying to lead a breakout attempt in his KV-1 tank. The hastily planned Soviet counter-offensive was another costly failure, costing the Bryansk Front 30,000 casualties and the loss of 123 tanks, but von Weichs was forced to keep substantial reserves to protect the left flank of his army group.

Despite repeated failures, Stavka demanded that the Bryansk and Voronezh fronts mount a new counter-offensive in August. Rather than logically looking for weak points in Heeresgruppe B's defensive line – which clearly lay in the sector south of Voronezh held by the Hungarian Second Army – Stavka once again ordered unimaginative attacks against the strongest point of the enemy line. Rokossovsky (Bryansk Front commander) and Vatutin (Voronezh Front commander) were two of the Red Army's most capable operational-level commanders, but they were constantly goaded into ill-considered efforts by Stalin, who chose to ignore basic planning factors like terrain, logistics and the enemy situation. Consequently, Group Chibisov mounted another futile frontal assault against VII.Armee-Korps on 12 August, which the Germans shut down within a few days. Amazingly, the Soviets made only small efforts to harass the Hungarian Second Army, even though the lightly equipped Hungarians were highly vulnerable. The Voronezh Front's 6th Army managed to gain three small bridgeheads across the Don in the Hungarian sector, the most significant of which were at Uryv and Korotoyak, 60–70km south of Voronezh. The 6th Army pushed the 25th

Italian *Bersaglieri* on the Eastern Front. In the foreground, a team operates a Breda M37 8mm heavy machine gun. The 3rd Cavalry Division (PADA) had six battalions of *Bersaglieri*, who were supposed to have better training and initiative than standard line infantry units. As 6.Armee advanced east to Stalingrad, Italian divisions began occupying screening positions along the Don. (Nik Cornish@www.stavka.org)

Guards Rifle Division into Uryv, which the Hungarian III Corps attacked on 18 July and then again on 10 August; the Hungarian attacks ended in failure, with heavy losses. The Soviet 174th Rifle Division crossed the Don at Korotoyak on 5 August and mauled the Hungarian 10th Light Infantry Division. Pushed by von Weichs to eliminate these pesky Soviet toeholds across the Don, the Hungarian IV Corps committed another division to launch a counter-attack, but the 12th Light Infantry Division suffered crippling losses in the effort. Eventually, the Hungarians committed their 1st Armoured Division to reduce the Korotayak bridgehead and the Germans sent an infantry regiment and some artillery. However, neither the Uryv nor Korotayak bridgeheads were eliminated until September.

Russian sources have claimed then – and now – that the fighting around Voronezh tied down significant forces from Heeresgruppe B and inflicted heavy losses on the enemy; these claims are partially correct. During July and August, 2.Armee suffered over 27,000 casualties, including 6,900 dead and missing, which diverted a substantial amount of replacements away from Paulus and Hoth. In addition, the Hungarian Second Army suffered over 14,000 casualties along the Don in July and August. However, Soviet losses were an order of magnitude higher, and von Weichs was actually able to thin out German forces along much of the Don and achieve an economy of force. The veteran 9. and 11.Panzer divisions were transferred to Heeresgruppe Mitte in August, leaving von Weichs' left wing and centre with no significant mobile reserves – but he was still able to hold off multiple counter-offensives by numerically superior enemy forces. At the end of August, only three German infantry divisions were supporting the Hungarian Second and Italian Eighth armies. If anyone was pinned down, it was the mass of Soviet armour around Voronezh, which could have been used more profitably elsewhere.

Gariboldi's Italian Eighth Army was also highly vulnerable along the Don, which Eremenko recognized. Unknown to him, the Germans had suspended fuel deliveries to the Eighth Army and the Italian artillery was desperately short of ammunition. After the German victory in the Don Bend, Eremenko sought to divert Paulus from marching directly upon Stalingrad by nipping at his flanks. General-leytenant Vasiliy I. Kuznetsov's 63rd Army was ordered to attack the Italian XXXV Corps, in conjunction with the 21st Army attacking the left flank of the German XVII.Armee-Korps. However, this offensive was to be conducted with only local resources, which limited its ability to inflict damage. On 20 August, the 63rd Army attacked across the Don with two rifle divisions and gained a bridgehead by pushing back the Italian Sforzesca Division. However, the simultaneous attack with two rifle divisions from the 21st Army was less successful. Kuznetsov slowly expanded his bridgehead at Yelanskaya, adding in another rifle division and his only mobile reserve, the 3rd Guards Cavalry Corps. However, the Germans refused to provide any reinforcements – even Luftwaffe support – to this sector, and told Gariboldi to clear up the situation with his own resources. Gariboldi committed his only mobile reserve, the Italian 3rd Cavalry Division (PADA), to begin a counter-attack against the Soviet bridgehead. Yet before the Italians could act, Kuznetsov's 63rd Army launched a major effort on 25 August to expand its bridgehead, spearheaded by the 3rd Guards Cavalry Corps and the 14th Guards Rifle Division. The Italian XXXV Corps was driven back 10km and the line nearly broken; if Kuznetsov had possessed a single brigade of T-34s, the Italians would have been in serious trouble. The lightly equipped 3rd Cavalry Division (PADA) had difficulty stopping even Soviet infantry, and the arrival of the Barbo Cavalry Brigade was of slight help. Finally, Kuznetsov's offensive ran out of steam by the end of August, and the Italians were able to stabilize their line. However, the Soviets were left with a significant bridgehead across the Don in a poorly defended sector, which would spell real trouble for Heeresgruppe B later in the campaign.

The Hungarian 1st Armoured Division had a reconnaissance battalion equipped with 14 39M Csaba armoured cars. The 6.4-ton Csaba was a fairly modern design, and equipped with a 20mm anti-tank gun. The Hungarian armoured division was kept as a mobile reserve near Voronezh and was used – unsuccessfully – to counter-attack Soviet bridgeheads across the Don in August and September 1942. (Nik Cornish@ www.stavka.org)

EREMENKO GAINS A BRIDGEHEAD, 20 AUGUST 1942 (PP. 86–87)

In an effort to divert German forces away from Stalingrad, General-polkovnik Andrei I. Eremenko – the newly appointed commander of the Stalingrad Front – decided to launch two attacks along the Don River. One blow was launched by the 63rd Army and 21st Army against the boundary of the German XVII.Armee-Korps and Italian XXXV Corps, while the other attack was conducted by the 1st Guards Army near Kletskaya. Unlike earlier Soviet counter-attacks, none of these attacks received any significant armour, artillery or air support. Nevertheless, the Italian Sforzesca Division, which had been assigned to hold the Yelanskaya–Rybinsky sector, was poorly prepared for defence. The Italians had only occupied this sector on the south bank of the Don four days before the Soviet offensive began, and the 30km front was more than double what a division could effectively defend. Furthermore, the Italian supporting artillery had very little ammunition, and the Germans had also decided to suspend fuel deliveries to the entire Italian Eighth Army in order to prioritize fuel for their own 6.Armee.

The Soviet 63rd Army began crossing the Don on a wide front on the morning of 20 August, with two division-size shock groups. After a brief artillery barrage, the 14th Guards Rifle Division began crossing the 200m-wide Don in small boats and rubber rafts. On the opposite bank, Italian troops from the 54th Infantry Regiment held only a few widely spaced strongpoints, and lacked the firepower to oppose the Soviet crossing. Once 14th Guards Rifle Division had sufficient troops across the river, it began pushing southwards, overrunning the Italian positions. On the first day of the attack, 14th Guards Rifle Division advanced only 3km but gained a solid lodgement, which was expanded over the next week. The Germans dispatched no reinforcements to aid the Italians and the Sforzesca Division was roughly handled, suffering over 1,000 casualties.

In this scene, Soviet infantry (1) are overrunning the Italian positions overlooking the Don and taking their first prisoners (2). Casualties from both sides are evident, and sporadic artillery fire is landing in the area. In the background, the next wave of Soviet boats are crossing the river (3).

Although the 63rd Army's advance was eventually stopped, and no German units were sent to reinforce this sector, Eremenko had gained a valuable bridgehead over the Don – which would be of great value in the next few months.

ANALYSIS

The nine-week advance to Stalingrad cost Paulus' 6.Armee over 40,000 casualties, including 10,314 dead or missing. When Hoth's 4.Panzer-Armee is included, total German casualties in the main strike force exceeded 50,000, or roughly 10 per cent of the committed forces. Material losses were also fairly debilitating, particularly in the Panzer and assault gun units, although damaged vehicles could be repaired or replaced given an operational pause. The main German trump card remained the Luftwaffe, which had gained near complete air superiority over the Stalingrad region.

In retrospect, *Blau* was a historic gamble, made with desperately thin margins. Hitler's ambition to achieve a decisive operational-level success in southern Russia was frustrated more by logistic problems at the front than any other factor. Time and again, German mechanized spearheads were brought to a halt by fuel and ammunition shortages, just as opportunities for decisive success presented themselves. The main problem facing Paulus was that he was not advancing along rail lines towards the Volga, which meant that the distance to the nearest railheads became insurmountable for his supply columns. Luftwaffe aerial resupply prevented a real disaster from occurring, but was insufficient to support 6.Armee in the field – a lesson that was conveniently forgotten as summer ended.

In operational terms, Heeresgruppe B's performance during July and August 1942 was bold and effective on both the offense and defence, although the level of risk-taking was exceedingly high. Heeresgruppe B was able to demolish the first two Soviet tank armies and achieved lopsided victories in almost every tank battle. While Paulus' operational decision-making was problematic at times, he still managed to fulfill most of *Blau*'s original objectives by late August. At the tactical level, the Germans benefitted from excellent leadership and realistic training, enabling them to bounce back from adversity, even when spearhead units found themselves isolated and nearly out of supply.

In contrast, the Soviet performance during the initial stages of *Blau* was uninspiring. Despite the availability of very strong armoured reserves, the Bryansk Front managed to lose Voronezh to a coup

Unable to capture all of Stalingrad in a coup de main, 6.Armee now had to prepare for a deliberate assault to overrun the Soviet defences in the city. In the meantime, German units were increasingly drawn into urban combat, which had not been part of the *Blau* plan. (Nik Cornish@www.stavka.org)

A knocked-out T-34 Model 1942 in northern Stalingrad, August 1942. The city's defenders used their remaining armour to anchor strongpoints and to support local counter-attacks. Now began the great ordeal of the Red Army – the protracted defence of Stalingrad, waiting for winter to neutralize the German superiority in air support. (Author's collection)

de main, then bungled one counter-attack after another against Heeresgruppe B. Timoshenko's South-Western Front avoided total destruction, saving some remnants to fight another day, but it could do little except retreat in front of the enemy juggernaut. Much of the Red Army's problems during the opening weeks of the campaign were caused by direct interference from Stalin and Stavka, trying to micromanage operations and relieving commanders who failed to achieve unrealistic objectives. Stalin's insistence upon committing entire armies to offensive operations with minimal planning or preparation was a recipe for disaster, but it was symptomatic of a regime that demanded results without regard to costs. Soviet personnel losses in trying to stop Heeresgruppe B in July and August were over 400,000, including 170,000 Soviet prisoners, and nearly 2,000 tanks were lost or disabled. Based upon the Soviet operational-level performance demonstrated in July and August, there was nothing to indicate that either the Voronezh or Stalingrad fronts had learned much from their failed counter-offensives. Indeed, the next round of Soviet offensives would employ the same flawed methods.

Yet, at the tactical level, it was clear that Soviet defensive resistance was increasing in August 1942 and that Heeresgruppe B was beginning to incur heavy losses to secure objectives. The commitment of more Guards units was part of the reason for increased defensive capabilities, along with veteran commanders. Although Stalin was quick to relieve commanders for failure,

As the situation at Stalingrad stagnated, Paulus was obliged to shift units to defend his left flank from Soviet counter-attacks. Here, 100.Jäger-Division moves towards the Kremenskaya sector, to block the 1st Guards Army, which has a bridgehead over the Don. (Author's collection)

he ensured that the Red Army's best commanders were sent to the Voronezh–Stalingrad sectors: Eremenko, Chuikov, Moskalenko and Shumilov were all competent leaders. In addition, the regime used a potent mix of propaganda and terror to build the will to fight in the common soldiers; the Germans were slow to recognize it, but the Soviet soldier was evolving into a much tougher opponent than the cannon fodder of 1941.

The Soviets did make two significant operational mistakes during the initial stages of the campaign, which enabled Paulus to reach Stalingrad. First, Stavka's decision to establish a defensive line forward of the Don, to shield Stalingrad, invited encirclement. The deployment of the 62nd and 64th armies was conducted in a wasteful manner that was not based upon sound defensive principles. Had the 62nd and 64th armies established a solid defensive line behind the Don, it is hard to imagine how Heeresgruppe B could have penetrated this line without great difficulty. Second, the decision to commit virtually all of the Stalingrad Front's armoured reserves to try to rescue this defensive line once it was threatened with encirclement deprived Eremenko of the resources to respond forcefully to any unexpected German breakthroughs. If Eremenko had still possessed an intact 1st Tank Army in mid-August, this powerful reserve could have been used to counter-attack any German bridgeheads across the Don or fend off flanking efforts by Hoth. Instead, Eremenko's cupboard was nearly bare by the time that Hube's panzers reached the city's outskirts, forcing him to resort to naval infantry and militia to help hold a critical facility like the STZ. By early September 1942, the Soviets were playing for time at Stalingrad, hoping to hold on long enough for more substantial reinforcements to arrive. Yet, the outlook on 3 September was that Stalingrad would likely fall in the next few weeks.

The Soviets pour reinforcements into Stalingrad, beginning a battle of attrition for the city. Contrary to some film portrayals, the Soviet troops sent to Stalingrad were not mere cannon fodder, but included some quality Guards units from Stavka reserves. (Author's collection)

THE BATTLEFIELD TODAY

The memorial to the defenders of the Shilovo bridgehead, south of Voronezh. The memorial commemorates the sacrifice of the 232nd Rifle Division and 18th Tank Corps in trying to block Hoth's panzers from reaching the city in early July 1942. A total of 969 Russian soldiers are buried here. (Author's collection)

Anyone wishing to visit the initial battlefields of *Fall Blau* should consider starting in Voronezh. The city is served primarily by domestic airlines, and visitors will likely have to change flights in Moscow, then endure Aeroflot for the 1½-hour flight to Voronezh. The city makes for a good base of operations, since it is replete with modern hotels, public transport and rental cars. During 1942 and 1943, an estimated 92 per cent of all residential buildings in the city were destroyed, and in 2008, the Russian government recognized the sacrifices made in its defence by conferring the title of 'city of military glory' upon Voronezh. The main memorial complex, located in the city centre on the west bank of the Voronezh River, is the site of a mass grave for about 15,000 Soviet soldiers killed in the defence of Voronezh in 1942 and 1943. A bas-relief of a dying Soviet soldier is particularly poignant and backed by tablets that list names of 3,535 of the known fallen. As customary in Russian memorials, a 40m-tall plinth, topped with a Russian eagle, provides the centrepiece of the complex. Victory Square, adjoining the memorial, boasts traditional red granite, an eternal flame and patriotic statutes (which include the proper mix of soldiers, partisans and collective workers). Nearby, a separate memorial, known as Peschanyy Log, commemorates the execution of 452 local residents by the Germans in August 1942. The most interesting memorial is located near the village of Shilovo, 12km south of the city, to honour the sacrificial defence of the 232nd Rifle Division.

Another item of interest located near the memorial complex is the Arsenal Museum of World War II, which is actually a fairly modern military history museum and attempts to showcase events that occurred around Voronezh in 1942 and 1943. The Arsenal Museum offers a life-size replica of a Soviet command bunker, various dioramas, some World War II

equipment from both sides and plenty of photos. However, the museum is not geared to foreign visitors, and all exhibits are exclusively in Russian. Another facility, the Diorama Museum on the east side of the Voronezh River, has some unremarkable outdoor displays, mostly a mix of late World War II and Cold War armoured vehicles. Like most World War II exhibits in Russia, the purpose of most of the memorials in or around Voronezh is to recognize Soviet sacrifices and victory over Fascism, not to provide historically accurate campaign narratives.

Outside Voronezh, many of the towns occupied by Heeresgruppe B in the initial push towards the Don, such as Gorshechnoye, Kastornoye and Stary Oskol, have small military cemeteries and monuments, to commemorate the casualties of 1941–43. A number of smaller monuments to individuals and some units can also be found around these towns, if one has patience and a local guide. The town of Rossosh has a well-kept military cemetery, which actually includes the remains of both German and Soviet soldiers – almost unheard of in Russia. Just to the north-west of Kalach, on Hill 169.4, there is a memorial for the 13th Tank Corps and its counter-attack against 6.Armee in July 1942; this site has a IS-2 heavy tank and graves of some of the Soviet tankers lost in nearby fighting. One of the more interesting memorials is for 'Kochetkov's 16 Guardsmen' on Hill 180.9, located 2km west of Sirotinskaya. Although few signs of the campaign are apparent, here and there, along either side of the Don, some fieldworks are still evident even after almost 80 years.

Of course, there are plenty of monuments in Volgograd – which will be discussed more in the next volume. In the northern suburbs, there are monuments marking the sacrifice of both the 1077th Anti-Aircraft Regiment gunners and the naval infantrymen. Although many foreign tourists visit Volgograd, most memorials in the city are designed to kindle Russian nationalism with displays that evoke sacrifice for Mother Russia and eventual victory. These kind of jingoistic displays appeal to modern mythologizing about World War II, but they also ignore the fact that the Soviet Union was in desperate straits in late August 1942 and was faced with the very real prospect of defeat at Stalingrad.

A T-34 tank is recovered from the Don River in July 2016. A KV-1 tank was recovered from the Don in 2014, and an American-made Stuart light tank in 2017. None of these tanks' ammunition or crews remain aboard, suggesting that they were deliberately driven into the river to avoid capture. In any case, Russian teams continue to recover various items of battlefield detritus, even nearly 80 years after the conclusion of *Blau*. (Author's collection)

FURTHER READING

Primary sources

Lagenkarten, AOK II, 1942, NAM (National Archives Microfilm), Series T-312, Rolls 1206

Kriegstagebuch (KTB), O. Qu., Panzerarmee 4, 1942, NAM (National Archives Microfilm), Series T-313, Roll 351

Kriegstagebuch (KTB), LV.Armee-Korps, 1942, NAM (National Archives Microfilm), Series T-314, Roll 1372

FMS D-139, Transportation in Russia

Secondary sources

Bergstrom, Christer et al., *Black Cross, Red Star: Air War over the Eastern Front*, Vol. 3, Hamilton, MT: Eagle Editions Ltd., 2006

Chuikov, Vasily I., *The Battle for Stalingrad*, New York: Holt, Reinhart and Winston, 1964

Donohue, Alan P., 'Operation *KREML*: German Strategic Deception on the Eastern Front in 1942', in *Weaving the Tangled Web* (ed. Christopher M. Rein), Fort Leavenworth, KS: Army University Press, 2018

Gerbet, Klaus (ed.), *Generalfeldmarschall Fedor von Bock: The War Diary, 1939–1945*, Atglen, PA: Schiffer Publishing Ltd., 1996

Glantz, David M., *To the Gates of Stalingrad: Soviet–German Combat Operations, April–August 1942,* Lawrence, KS: University Press of Kansas, 2009

Golikov, Filipp I., боях за Воронеж [*The Battle for Voronezh*], Voronezh: Central Black Book Publishing House, 1968

Grinko, Aleksandr, В боях за Воронеж [*In the battles for Voronezh*] (Voronezh: Central Black Book Publishing House, 1985).

Halder, Franz, *The Halder War Diary, 1939–1942*, Novato, CA: Presidio Press, 1988

Hayward, Joel S. A., *Stopped at Stalingrad: The Luftwaffe and Hitler's Defeat in the East 1942–43*, Lawrence, KS: University Press of Kansas, 1998

Orenstein, Harold S., 'Combat operations of Briansk and Voronezh front forces in summer 1942 on the Voronezh axis', *The Journal of Slavic Military Studies*, Vol. 6, No. 2, 1993

Scianna, Bastian Matteo, *The Italian War on the Eastern Front, 1941–1943: Operations, Myths and Memories*, Switzerland: Palgrave Macmillan, 2019

Sdvizhkov, Igor, *Confronting Case Blue: Briansk Front's Attempt to Derail the German Drive to the Caucasus, July 1942*, Solihull: Helion & Company Ltd., 2017

Table of ranks

US Army rank	German Army rank	Soviet rank
General of the Army	Generalfeldmarschall	Marshal Sovetskogo Soyuza (Marshal of the Soviet Union)
General	Generaloberst	General Armiyi
Lieutenant-General	General der (Infanterie)	General-polkovnik
Major-General	Generalleutnant	General-leytenant
Brigadier-General	Generalmajor	General-major
Colonel	Oberst	Polkovnik
Lieutenant-Colonel	Oberstleutnant	Podpolkovnik
Major	Major	Major
Captain	Hauptmann	Kapetan
1st Lieutenant	Oberleutnant	Starshiy-leytenant
2nd Lieutenant	Leutnant	Mladshiy-leytenant
Master Sergeant	Oberfeldwebel	Starshina
Technical Sergeant	Feldwebel	Starshiy-serzhant
Staff Sergeant	Unterfeldwebel	
Sergeant	Unteroffizier	Serzhant
Corporal		Mladshiy-serzhant
Private First Class	Obergefreiter	Yefreytor

INDEX

Figures in bold refer to illustrations.